IMAGES
of America

SISTER BAY
WISCONSIN

Although it was a rural farm community, the Village of Sister Bay, since its earliest days, projected an impression of elegance. The word was not found in any early, or even recent, literature about the community, but it is more than evident in many of the photographs that were taken in the earlier days. The above greeting card was mailed almost a century ago, and the glistening speckles of gold and silver still reflect from the three-dimensional card that was sent through the mails. (Courtesy of the *Door County Advocate*.)

IMAGES

of America

SISTER BAY
WISCONSIN

Joseph W. Zurawski

ARCADIA
PUBLISHING

Published by Arcadia Publishing
Charleston, South Carolina

Library of Congress Catalog Card Number: Applied for

For all general information contact Arcadia Publishing at:
Telephone 843-853-2070
Fax 843-853-0044
E-mail sales@arcadiapublishing.com
For customer service and orders:
Toll-Free 1-888-313-2665

Visit us on the Internet at www.arcadiapublishing.com

John R. Greene Jr., pours the champagne and congratulates John Blossom on winning the annual "regatta" conducted between the families on Green Bay, just off Sister Bay. Both families own shorefront property in Sister Bay, and the "regatta" tradition has lasted for a good part of a century when both families first bought land in Sister Bay. Numerous other families have been regularly visiting Sister Bay over the past century, many remaining for the entire summer. (Courtesy of John R. Green Jr.)

CONTENTS

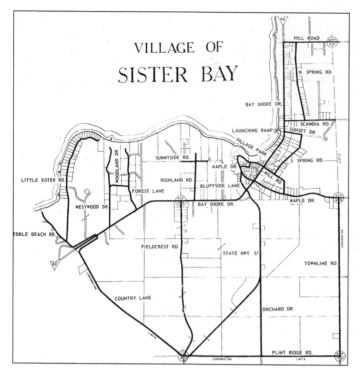

VILLAGE OF
SISTER BAY

The Village of Sister Bay has grown to an area of 2.58 square miles and 1,651 acres in 1999, an increase of less than 100 acres from the time the village was incorporated in 1912. Eight hundred sixteen acres were designated for single family and multiple family residences. Two hundred sixty acres were to be utilized by general, resort, and highway commercial, with the central business district occupying five percent of the area. The remainder of the land was classified as agricultural or open spaces. This map depicts the major roadways of the Village of Sister Bay. (Courtesy of the Zielke Family Archives.)

ACKNOWLEDGMENTS

I would like to thank the following individuals who have helped make this book possible. Many shared with me their photos, their stories, their time, and their love for a community that holds a special place in their hearts.

Jay Blossom, John Blossom, Allen Brodd, Robert Berns, Clyde Casperson, Anita Conlon (St. Rosalia Church Archives), Helen D. Carlson, Emilie Daubner, Sharon Daubner, Allen Erickson, Tonda Gagliardo, John R. Greene Jr., Mary Alice Gustafson, Paul Hulbert, George Jischke, Lon Kopitzke (*Door Reminder*), Mary Ann Guterman, Jane Harberg (Sister Bay Moravian Church Archives), John R. Henry, Lars Johnson, Jane Kayser, Dorothy Laaksonen, Phyllis Larson, Richard Malmgren, George (Pat) Mangan (Transfiguration of Our Lord Archives), Susan Mathey, Harry A. Muller, Catherine L. Peot (Archives of the First Baptist Church of Sister Bay), Kathy Ray, Thomas Sadler (Sister Bay Historical Society), Richard Scheller, JoAnn Thomas, John Vieth, Village of Sister Bay, Betty L Wiltse, and Terry R. and Linda Zielke.

Idalia Ortiz not only typed the manuscript but also made many helpful suggestions. Patrick Catel and Keith Ulrich of Arcadia Publishing helped guide this work from the idea stage to publication.

Joseph W. Zurawski

INTRODUCTION

The Village of Sister Bay is located in northern Door County, Wisconsin. With an official population of some seven hundred, it is the second largest community of residents on the 90-mile Door County peninsula.

Statistics can be deceptive. When Al Johnson's, a popular restaurant, opens at 6:00 a.m. during the summer, it may well serve 3,000 anxious diners before it closes. That number could be higher if more diners choose to wait more than an hour. And there often are waiting periods at the dozen other places one might dine in Sister Bay.

The Catholic church in town, St. Rosalia's, has a weekly service for its two hundred parishioners. On a summer weekend, perhaps as many as 1,500 will fill its pews at four or five services. In cold weather, the newly constructed church closes its two wings built exclusively to handle the summer visitors.

The fall festival somehow manages to accommodate 10,000 or more visitors per day on one two-lane highway that stretches approximately 2 miles through the community.

One might suspect that Sister Bay had a charmed or storied historical background that helped to create its appeal to so many visitors. A brief review of the actual history of Sister Bay suggests otherwise. The name "Sister Bay" was given to the area by Increase Claflin, an early resident-explorer of Door County. Claflin, generally acknowledged as the first permanent white resident of Door County, named the islands near today's Sister Bay and Little Sister Bay as the Sister Islands, because they seemed to resemble each other as sisters often do.

Little Sister Bay began to emerge as a settlement before Sister Bay. By 1857, a pier was built to accommodate ships. There was a store, a blacksmith shop, and a saloon. A ship arrived in 1865 with the crew suffering from diphtheria. All died except one crew member, and a sheep pasture was converted into a cemetery to bury the dead. There was little interest afterwards in further development of the area of Little Sister Bay. Attention turned northward to the area of today's Sister Bay. The entire area, at this time, was known as the town of Liberty Grove.

In 1857, John Thoreson was the first settler in Little Sister Bay. He established a general store, but left the town in the 1880s. Ingebret Tergeson, also a Norwegian, settled in today's area of Sister Bay, building a cabin on a hill that was the site of the County House Resort more than a century later. James Hanson, another Norwegian, and Christian Hempel, a Prussian, also arrived in 1857. Hanson was a merchant while Hempel took up farming, as did Byron Aslagson, a Norwegian, who arrived in 1858. Other early settlers included Peter Josephson, Hans Gunnerson, Endre Enderson (Anderson), Moses Thompson, Charles Gros, and John Rogers.

With the arrival of Pat and Thomas Dimond in 1869, the nucleus of the first commercial business in the Sister Bay area began to emerge. In 1870, the firm of Henderson, Coon, and Dimond constructed the first commercial pier and sawmill.

An organizational meeting for the Board of Trustees for the Village of Sister Bay was conducted April 23, 1912. Sister Bay was formally incorporated at this time. Ole Erickson, Frank Bunda, Charles Kellstrom, Ed Koessl Sr., Adolph Roeser, Matt Roeser, and John Pahl were trustees for the new village. A budget of $200 was adopted for the year. Concern was expressed about the conditions of roads within the city.

Disaster struck Sister Bay several times in 1912. A fire, believed to have been caused by lightning, almost destroyed the village. Six commercial buildings burned including the Sister Bay Hotel and the old home of Andre Roeser. After the fire, a severe drought resulted in the loss of livestock and massive crop failures. Then came the invasion of grasshoppers that darkened the sky as they swarmed, destroying what little crops survived the drought. A hailstorm leveled what was left of the fields.

Andre Roeser was an influential businessman in the Sister Bay area from the time he arrived in 1877 to his death in 1915. He built a commercial pier, launched a sawmill and lumberyard, operated a flour mill, ran a tugboat service, and had an icehouse. Roeser also had a 15-room boarding house that served as a hotel. Rates were $1.50 per day, which included three meals and laundry service. The Roeser home was the social center of the town. Before a Catholic church could be built, Roeser set aside a large room, 18 feet by 30 feet, where Mass was celebrated every month for more than 20 years. In the early 1890s, Roeser gave some land in Sister Bay to the Diocese of Green Bay so that a Catholic church could be built. It opened as St. Rosalia's Church a few years later. Roeser was also the Sister Bay agent for the Goodrich Steamship lines. The Roeser pier and mills were located at the site of today's Sister Bay Resort and Yacht Club.

Other businesses in early Sister Bay were the dry goods store of Mrs. Wenzel Bunda, the hardware store of John Pahl, Casper Nye's implement store operated by Henry Star, Lerner's, a men's clothing store, the Sister Bay Hotel, and Frank Jischke's meat market.

Hard drinking in Sister Bay did not meet with the approval of the very active Baptist community, which formally organized a church in 1877 with 14 charter members. Members of the church were influential in having the Sister Bay area declared "dry" for a short period. However, once the town voted to stay "wet" it has been so since the village was incorporated. A Sunday School, a vacation bible school, a men's choir, a women's sewing club and later a choir, were but a few of the many active groups associated with the Swedish Baptist Church, which later changed its name to the First Baptist Church of Sister Bay. The Moravian Church and the Lutheran Church, both still active in today's community, were organized around the turn of the century.

For almost a century the Liberty Grove Hotel, Liberty Park Summer Resort, the Hotel DuNord, and the Little Sister Resort have been attracting hundreds of visitors annually. Today these hotels are still in operation. They are joined by a dozen others who welcome thousands of visitors every week during the summer and fall months.

During these months, there seems to be a flurry of continual activity along the town's main street, Highway 42 or Bay Shore Drive, from sunrise to sunset. Parking is at a premium; everyone seems to be shopping, going for a bite to eat, getting ready for a sail, or simply strolling comfortably along Green Bay's shore or down the street.

Still one must pause and closely observe. There is not one billboard to be seen. In fact, Sister Bay censured itself, claiming that the sign welcoming visitors to the village was too big. As well, one can look further at the Sister Islands. A few years ago, there was a move to commercialize them, but commercial they would not be. Sister Bay acted, and the Sister Islands will remain as they were when they were named some 150 years ago—a habitat for birds and wildlife.

No matter how much activity or how many people, there never seems to be an anxious moment in Sister Bay. A serene tranquil quality is a way of life for residents and appreciated by visitors.

Although there has been some concern about the pollution brought to the region by the thousands of vehicles in the area, the magic that is Sister Bay will no doubt continue to attract more visitors, and probably summer residents, in the future. Those living in Sister Bay and those simply visiting may just be able to continue to believe that Sister Bay will continue to "grow" and remain unchanged well into the future.

One

Geographic Setting

I.A.C. Graves, surveyor, was commissioned in 1911 to complete a survey of the proposed Village of Sister Bay. He presented his survey showing the corporate limits of the proposed village that would include 1,558 acres as shown in the plat at right, which is available for viewing in the archives of the Sister Bay Historical Society.

Driftwood on the white pebble beach
of Little Sister Bay
Sister Bay, Wisconsin.

Attempts at settlement, mostly unsuccessful, in the area known as Little Sister Bay were continually made during the last third of the nineteenth century. The above photo, taken around 1900, shows driftwood, perhaps from shipwrecks or commercial sawmill operations, on White Pebble Beach in Little Sister Bay. White Pebble Beach is the furthest inward point of Little Sister Bay. (Courtesy of the Sister Bay Historical Society.)

This is another view of Little Sister Bay with White Pebble Beach on the extreme right. The white building is the boathouse at Little Sister Resort and the docking facilities. The photo was probably taken a few years after the Little Sister Resort was established in 1918 by Grant Anderson. Today, the area is more often referred to as "Pebble Beach." (Courtesy of Mary Alice Gustafson.)

A view of Sister Bay around 1913 is pictured above. St. Rosalia's Catholic Church, on the left, is shown at the bottom of the hill before it was rebuilt on the top of the hill. What was to become today's Highway 42 is shown merging with today's Highway 57 several hundred feet east of where the two main roads to Sister Bay merge today. (Courtesy of Allen and Bonnie Brodd.)

This photo was probably taken in the early 1900s and shows a view of Sister Bay looking south toward the Sister Bay Hotel on the left. The Bunda store and the Louis Lerner store are on the right. The mounds of cord along the side of the hotel were probably there in preparation for the winter season. The road pictured is today's Highway 42, and the incline at the extreme southern end of town, in the center of the photo, appears to be much flatter than it is today. (Courtesy of the Kathy Ray Collection.)

Sister Bay's early school was located on a hill near today's Highway 57 near the approach to the village on the southern end. St. Rosalia's Church is visible on the left. Today, the school is the Northern Door County Day Care Center, and the church is the Mission Grille Restaurant. The above photo, which shows much less vegetation than is around the restaurant today, suggests that the area on the extreme left of the photo was not as hilly as it is today. (Courtesy of Mary Alice Gustafson.)

This photo depicts the Gust Carlson farm, east of Sister Bay, on today's Scandia Road around 1913. Carlson was also a carpenter. On the photo his farm is identified as a "California Farm," perhaps because of the variety of fruits and vegetables that were harvested. (Courtesy of Allen and Bonnie Brodd.)

This is a view of Sister Bay from the bluff at the southeast corner of the village, above today's location of the Village View Motel, facing northwest. Joe Hendrickson's house is on the far right. The Sister Bay Hotel is in the center, along with Husby's Blacksmith Shop, which became Husby's Implement Sales around 1910—the date of this photo. (Courtesy of the Kathy Ray Collection.)

This is a view of Sister Bay in 1913. It shows the downtown area where six buildings were completely destroyed by fire in 1912. The Sister Bay Hotel is the large building on the right. It is more than twice the size of the previous Sister Bay Hotel that occupied the same site. Although it appears well in the distance, the Roeser home, center background, still reflects the imposing presence it had in early Sister Bay. (Courtesy of Allen and Bonnie Brodd.)

This is a view of Clark Street, today's Maple Street, looking east from the area of the Roeser dock. The Roeser residence, the largest building in Sister Bay, is on the extreme right. The building was sold to Clarence and Laura Brodd in 1926, and then in 1946 to Joe and Ethel Kwaterski who remodeled it into an apartment building. (Courtesy of the Sister Bay Historical Society.)

There were continual promotions encouraging visitors and vacationers to come to Sister Bay. The above postal card, prepared around 1910–1915, depicts Rowleys Bay. It states "Raleigh's Bay, near Sister Bay." Anyone coming to Sister Bay wishing to make a trip to Rowleys Bay at that time would have a difficult time reaching the location by road. Few autos were available, there was no bus service, and farmers would be too busy to take vacationers from one side of the peninsula to the other. Travel by boat was available by first going to Washington Island, about 15 miles north of Sister Bay. However, depending on how the wind blew, the ferry leaving Washington Island might just reach Gill's Rock on the western shore of Door County when it was attempting to reach Rowleys Bay, which is on the eastern shore of the peninsula. Wind and currents were very unpredictable and often shifted after ferries left Washington Island. The ferry captain had little choice but to navigate the way according to the dictates of the wind and current. (Courtesy of Mary Alice Gustafson.)

14

Birchwood Hall, a resort hotel, was built at the north end of Sister Bay in the heavily wooded area pictured above. It is located near today's Beach Road. Since the three areas are very hilly, farmers did not attempt to farm since many of the trees, which were there when the areas were settled, remain today. The above photo was taken during the 1920s. (Courtesy of Mary Alice Gustafson.)

This view is from the Birchwood Hall resort hotel, near today's Beach Road, west toward the waters of Green Bay—probably a few years after the hotel was built in 1909. Although the hotel wanted to retain as much privacy as possible, some of the trees appear to be removed to enhance the view from the hotel which "was built in a lower meadow," as a local author wrote, "surrounded by a lovely grove of cedars and pines." (Courtesy of the Sister Bay Historical Society.)

This photo was taken from an area of today's Highway 42, facing south about 1 mile north of the location of today's Door County Ice Cream Factory at the north end of Sister Bay, around 1920. On the right is Andrew Knudsen's farm where grain crops were grown. Mrs. Alice Gustafson, who lives in the area, remembers working with the threshing machines throughout the area. There were also dairy farms and milk for sale. "For many years," says Gustafson, "the farmers were anxious to get rid of the land along Green Bay and the shore. There just wasn't good farming there and they wanted to get inland." (Courtesy of Mary Alice Gustafson.)

The above picture is a view of today's Highway ZZ, at the time a dirt road, looking west into the Village of Sister Bay around 1915. The Lerner store is in the center with the Sister Bay Hotel on the right. (Courtesy of Mary Alice Gustafson.)

A viewing area of Sister Bay from Dr. Fickner's "Forest Ideal," located at the south end of Sister Bay behind the former site of St. Rosalia's Church, is pictured above. There was a retirement community on this location in the early years of the twentieth century. Later a restaurant and nursing home were built. (Courtesy of the Kathy Ray Collection.)

The owner of this photo believes it was taken in the 1890s of today's Sunset Drive facing east. There are no car tracks in the dirt road, and no buildings appear near or at the end of the road. (Courtesy of the Kathy Ray Collection.)

This is the first view of Sister Bay that visitors saw when coming from the south on Highway 42 in the 1930s. This scene depicts the top of the hill on the south end of Sister Bay looking north on today's Highway 42. Note the telephone poles on the right, which indicate where today's Highway 57 comes into Sister Bay and merges with Highway 42. (Courtesy of Mary Alice Gustafson.)

This view shows the entrance to Sister Bay during autumn, around 1950, on the south end of town where Highway 42 merges with Highway 57. Notice the guard rails that were installed since traffic was getting much heavier. On the left are five signs advertising the availability of motels in the area. Cars appear to be double-parked in front of Husby's, a popular restaurant and bar shown above on the left. On the right is a Lion's Club sign reflecting the quickly growing economic activity in the village. (Courtesy of Mary Alice Gustafson.)

This is the main street of Sister Bay, today's Highway 42—also known as Bay Shore Drive—looking north from the south end of the Village of Sister Bay, probably in the early 1950s. Salty Joe's Fish Market is on the left. The Texaco filling station is today's Henderson Park. (Courtesy of Mary Alice Gustafson.)

This is a view of Sister Bay probably from the 1950s. The two major highways, 42 and 57, are shown, lower left, just before they merge entering the town's business district. Several studies, including the one by the Bay-Lake Regional Planning Commission, identified the area as a "traffic hazard." However, the junction of these two roads remains heavily wooded, and comparing recent photos of the area with those almost a century old suggest that the incline just south of the junction is today much steeper than years ago. The same planning commission suggested a bypass of this area by auto traffic coming from the south. That plan was never put into effect, and virtually all traffic coming into Sister Bay passes through this point. (Courtesy of Mary Alice Gustafson.)

A good view of Sister Bay Bluff on the southern end of Sister Bay is shown above. On the right is the former Kellstrom dock with Charlie Kellstrom's boat *Flusheim*—used for fishing or giving sightseeing tours—at the dock. This site of the Kellstrom dock is the area of today's Sister Bay Marina. (Courtesy of the Kathy Ray Collection.)

Three docks were built on the shore at Helm's Haven Resort, today's Helm's Four Seasons, in 1959–1960, when a free rowboat was made available to everyone who rented a room or cottage. There was always a lot of activity along the Green Bay shore at that time, with the rowboats and other quickly improvised "vessels" made from logs "left over" from a local sawmill used for an afternoon on the bay, as well as huge seaweed fights, as a local businessman observed at the time. (Courtesy of the Zielke Family Archives.)

The docks of Sister Bay in 1978 are pictured above, starting at the southern end of the bay area. Sister Bay Resort and Yacht Club (lower left) Helm's Four Seasons (next right) the village park dock (next right) Al Johnson's dock (next right), and Clyde Casperson's dock (top right). Relative sizes can be determined according to the size of the Helm's dock, which was 70 feet out into the bay with a 60-foot diagonal addition. (Courtesy of the Zielke Family Archives.)

This is a view of the Berns Brothers Lumber Company of Sister Bay in 1958 when a new office building was added to the large area the company occupied on the southern end. Starting on the extreme left there was a lumber storage area, then the carpenter shop, a sawmill in the center, with the new office just above the sawmill. Retail sales and storage of coal and kegs of nails were located in the building in the lower center. On the right, rounded building, windows and doors were made and stored. Above that building, lifting machines were stored and maintained. The company, open year round, was most viable in the period between 1940 and 1970, and would guarantee delivery anywhere in Door County. The area today is the site of the Sister Bay Resort and Yacht Club. (Courtesy of the Robert Berns Collections.)

This is the Sister Bay Marina as it appeared in 1978, showing the 300-foot section added that year. When the marina opened in 1971, there were provisions for boats that could be accommodated in the 30 slips available. (Courtesy of the Village of Sister Bay.)

The Sister Bay Marina was completely rebuilt in 1993, with provisions for a minimum of one hundred boats. However, since some of the slips are 60 feet, as many as 155 boats can be docked. Approximately 35 slips are available for transient boaters. New break walls were installed in 1993, along with a new harbor master building. (Courtesy of the Village of Sister Bay.)

Two

Early Development

Lumber was the first established product of Sister Bay. The sawmill on the Roeser's dock in early Sister Bay is shown in the above photo on the left. After bark is removed from the logs, they are trimmed and stacked in front of the mill, and then specified amounts are placed on the dock (far right) to await shipment. The buildings between the two piles of logs are fish sheds. (Courtesy of Helen Carlson.)

There were three major fires at the mill on Roeser's dock in early Sister Bay. The above photo is believed to be a view of one of those fires. Cordwood, usually in sections 4 feet long (shown above) piled along the entire length of the dock, was used for building homes and boats. This mill, which had its own power plant, sawed logs and planed lumber. Horses were used to drag the lumber one log at a time. (Courtesy of the Robert Berns Collections.)

Around 1910, a major project was undertaken at the Roeser dock. A combination mill and product building was under construction, shown above, when a fire broke out and the complex burned to the ground. Had it been completed, it would have been the largest building ever constructed at the site until that time. (Courtesy of the Robert Berns Collections.)

The operations at Roeser dock around 1915 included the feed mill on the left. The mill had a steel shaft that was used to grind the feed. The steam engine was housed in the white building in the center. It contained a slide used to pull logs up into the building. The Everett B. Clarke Shipping Company is on the right. It sold seeds, as well as farm products such as peas and potatoes. (Courtesy of the Robert Berns Collections.)

The above photo shows the Roeser dock in Sister Bay. The big mound on the right is a coal delivery. Even though there was plenty of wood available, either as cordwood or from the waste of the sawmill operations, residents of Sister Bay burned large amounts of coal during winter, since coal was a much more efficient fuel than wood. (Courtesy of Mary Alice Gustafson.)

The feed mill at Roeser's dock in the 1930s, when it was owned by Elmer Berns, is pictured above. When it burned down for the third time, it was not rebuilt, and the area was used as a lumber mill and lumberyard. (Courtesy of the Robert Berns Collections.)

The Roeser home was more like a community hall than a personal residence in Sister Bay's early development. The presence of horses and carriages, not always belonging to residents of Sister Bay, would indicate a dance, party, funeral, or wedding (such as appears likely in the above photo) was taking place at the Roeser home. The largest building in Sister Bay, the Roeser residence had 15 rooms. The village's first post office and the first two general stores were set up in the basement. A creamery was operated in an adjoining building. The Roesers also owned a 1.5 miles of Green Bay shoreline. (Courtesy of the Sister Bay Historical Society.)

John W. Erickson had an ox team on his homestead in Sister Bay around 1885–1890, when it is believed this photo was taken. Several stories were told about this ox team. Once Sam Erickson, son of John, was driving the team and they went through the woods into the water of Green Bay and continued until only their nostrils could be seen. They had to be frightened back to shore. On another occasion, the team went through a driving rain to Baileys Harbor to return with a midwife. Sam's brother, August, was born a few hours later. (Courtesy of the Sister Bay Historical Society.)

This is the farm of Frank Logerquist, who moved there in 1908. He purchased it from John Logerquist, who purchased it from Rev. Charles Wassel, the first pastor to the Swedish Baptist Church, appointed in 1881. The farm of 69 acres was L-shaped and usually had eight to ten cows, several dozen chickens, some cherry trees, along with grain products. The cow barn is on the extreme left, and to the right is the granary, the outdoor toilet, windmill, residence, and chicken coop. The toilet was one of the conversation topics about the farm since it was very sturdy, and the Halloween pranksters could not tip it over as they did many others in the area. (Courtesy of Phyllis Larson.)

Ludwig Larson's dairy farm, just north of Sister Bay in the early twentieth century, is pictured above. The residence is on the extreme left, the granary in the center, with the windmill and barn on the right. There are numerous artesian wells beneath Sister Bay. Farmers would often have to drill several times for water before they struck one of these wells. (Courtesy of Phyllis Larson.)

This is the residence of Andrew Magnet and his family, who appear to be posing for the photo, in early Sister Bay. Barrels such as those by the picket fence were commonly used to catch and store rain water. The building was later the Sunstrom House owned by Willard Sunstrom, who also had some cottages built on the property near downtown Sister Bay. (Courtesy of Allen and Bonnie Brodd.)

The above is a photo of the Kellstrom homestead. Charlie and Anna had a large home on a farm where milk production was a top priority near the turn of the century. Even though there were always things to attend to on the farm, the word was that Charlie was always ready to go do some fishing. (Courtesy of the Kathy Ray Collection.)

The threshing machine would come to the farms of Sister Bay and move from farm to farm for about two to three weeks until all the oat and wheat seed were separated from the stalks. Neighbors would come together at one farm and remain, even if it meant sleeping overnight, until the entire crop was processed. Some believe that the thresher that worked the farms in Sister Bay was owned by Jake Kodanko's father. (Courtesy of the Sister Bay Historical Society.)

The Reynolds Preserving Company had numerous orchards throughout Door County. The above "bus," perhaps a redesigned truck, was used to transport workers from location to location. Notice the baby buggy near the front tire of the truck. The driver, who always stayed with his "bus," probably served as the babysitter while the mother was picking the harvest crop. (Courtesy of the Kathy Ray Collection.)

The Roeser Building on the right was a center for many social and business activities in the life of early Sister Bay and usually had more than the four people in the above photo bustling about. The street is identified as "Clarke," which is today's Maple Street. The building in the background was a wagon repair shop. The white building in the center was the residence of Casper Nyes. The buildings on the left were the residences of Wenzel Bunda and Edward Berns. (Courtesy of George Jischke.)

30

This is the main street—today's Highway 42—of Sister Bay in 1908. The building in the center was known as Koepsel's Dance Hall. It is the current Sister Bay Bowl. On the right is the former private residence of Casper Nyes, where Bill Berns had a barbershop. There was also a dental office upstairs. Today it is the Village View Motel. (Courtesy of George Jischke.)

This is an early view of Sister Bay, looking from the south to the far north end of the village. In the above photo, Andrew Hendrikson's and Edwin H. Casperson's residences are the two white buildings in the center background. Casperson's home was previously owned by Andrew Johnson. Barely noticeable, but also in white on the left side, is the Ole Erickson store and residence. (Courtesy of George Jischke.)

A good view of Frank Jischke's meat market (on the left) on Sister Bay's Clarke Street in the early twentieth century is pictured above. John Pahl's private residence is on the right. The fenced-in area was for the animals that almost all residents of the village owned. In early Sister Bay, maintenance of the roads was a major concern. What probably aided the situation was the requirement of all animals in the village to be fenced-in and not allowed to wander, especially after a heavy rainfall. (Courtesy of George Jischke.)

The store of John Pahl in Sister Bay was open for business in 1908. One source states that Pahl built the store, and another states that he purchased the building, and it took ten years for him and his wife, Emma, to pay for the property. Furniture and hardware were sold at the store. Emma supplemented the couple's income by sewing. Her specialty was sewing wedding gowns for which she was paid 75¢ per day. For her "everyday" sewing she charged 50¢ per day. However, while many of the less expensive customers failed to pay, her brides, Emma recalled, "always paid cash." She also raised chickens and did a lot of baking. John quickly became Sister Bay's banker, as he was always ready and willing to cash checks. He would frequently journey to Sturgeon Bay and return with hundreds of dollars, and he charged nothing for his check cashing service. During the Depression of 1929, when the banks failed throughout Door County, Emma had an account in a Kewaunee bank that was still solvent and helped the Pahls survive the economic Depression of the 1930s. (Courtesy of Allen and Bonnie Brodd.)

John Pahl is pictured here at his desk inside his furniture and hardware store in Sister Bay. There was only one major change in the store in the way that business was carried on for the 44 years between 1908 and 1952 that occurred when the Pahls retired. Electricity was installed in 1928. (Courtesy of the Sister Bay Historical Society.)

The Frank Bunda store in early Sister Bay was completely destroyed by fire, along with five other buildings, in the fire of 1912. An early account of the fire states, "after the empty building of Frank Smith's had become ignited from heat...the store building to the south, owned and occupied by Frank Bunda was next to catch fire...[after] the hotel had got a good start, the general store of Mrs. Wenzel Bunda, across from the Frank Bunda corner, caught so rapidly that no time was had to remove a thing." (Courtesy of the Sister Bay Historical Society.)

The general store of Mrs. W. Bunda is pictured above, along with the clothing store of Louis Lerner, in early Sister Bay. An auto is visible traveling south. This was a rare sight in Sister Bay at the time, as it is believed no autos were registered until the 1920s, a few years after this photo was taken. (Courtesy of Mary Alice Gustafson.)

This photo was taken inside Mrs. W. Bunda's store in early Sister Bay. Mrs. Bunda is on the left, Oscar Jacobson in the center rear, and Mary Bunda Jischke is on the right. The boxes on the left contained high-top boots. Numerous bolts of cloth were against the wall. The case held hatpins, men's pocket watches, and other smaller items. Much of the business was done on a barter system, with jars of butter or cartons of eggs often exchanged for some cloth, needles, or buttons. The first cash register could only calculate sales to $2.99. (Courtesy of the Kathy Ray Collection.)

34

The general store of Mrs. W. Bunda is shown here around 1907. This is a view looking south. The building on the left is the barbershop of Bill Berns—today's Village View Motel. The scene baffles many old-time residents, since they find it difficult to explain the absence of the steep decline on the southern end of Sister Bay today just as one enters the business district of the village. The above photo shows little of the decline. It is believed that the cabinet on the extreme right was used to drop off and pick up the mail. The Bunda store also served as the post office for Sister Bay. (Courtesy of George Jischke.)

After the fire of 1912 that destroyed the store of Mrs. W. Bunda on the corner of today's Maple Drive and Highway 42, the store was rebuilt and sold to Mrs. Bunda's son, William, who continued to operate the store until it burned to the ground in 1941. Because of World War II, the store was not immediately rebuilt. The Bunda business was carried on from the store known at the time as Eden's Bakery. (Courtesy of the Sister Bay Historical Society.)

This is a view looking north in early Sister Bay. The general store of Mrs. W. Bunda, with a young boy sitting on the front step, is on the left. The store of Louis Lerner, with a carriage and horse in front, is the store immediately across the street from the Sister Bay Hotel. The implements that were available for sale at a store and blacksmith shop are on the extreme right. Today that is the location of Jungwirth Hardware. (Courtesy of the Sister Bay Historical Society.)

This is a view of Sister Bay facing west around 1915. Starting from the right is the Sister Bay Hotel, across the street is Husby's, and behind that building is Jischke's meat market. On the other side of the street is the Berns residence, the Bunda Store, and the residence of Clarence Brodd. (Courtesy of the Sister Bay Historical Society.)

Ludwig and Hjalmer Seaquist are pictured above at a blacksmith shop in early Sister Bay. The shop was on the site that was to become the Lundquist Hardware Store, which occupied the area just south of the current Al Johnson's Restaurant. (Courtesy of the Sister Bay Historical Society.)

John Trucker was the owner and operator of a harness shop in the early days of Sister Bay. He had a thriving business that operated out of the Casperson building, which was located at the northern end of Sister Bay. Since the Casperson house jutted out across the proposed redesign of the highway to make it straight, that section was torn down when the highway was built. (Courtesy of the Sister Bay Historical Society.)

The banner covering the section of the awning that reads "Hayes Hardware Co." advertises a brand of stoves, which was being promoted at the store at the time with cooking demonstrations. This scene depicts early twentieth century Sister Bay. The Hayes Hardware store was located on today's Highway 42, north of the intersection of Maple Drive, near the site of a sign shop today that was previously the garage of a Shell Service station. (Courtesy of the Sister Bay Historical Society.)

Ole Erickson operated a general department and grocery store in early Sister Bay. He sold a variety of items including overalls, yarn goods, farm tools, and buckets. The store was located across the street from what is now Al Johnson's restaurant. Ole Erickson was active in the Republican Party and once was selected as a delegate to the National Republican Convention. (Courtesy of the Kathy Ray Collection.)

The original Sister Bay Hotel is pictured here before it burned down with several other buildings in 1912. The above scene suggests some type of commercial and community activity. A band is present to entertain, and numerous visitors arrived in autos. The milk wagon and what appear to be tubs of cheese indicate a commercial purpose for the vehicle's presence in the village. Note that the photo was taken from the interior of the store of Mrs. W. Bunda—several of the letters are evident in the upper left of the photo. (Courtesy of the Sister Bay Historical Society.)

Sister Bay suffered a devastating fire in 1912. Six buildings were destroyed in the central business district: the Lerner store, the Frank Bunda property, the Wenzel Bunda store, Henry Pleck's hotel, an empty saloon known as the Klondike, and the residence of Andrew Roeser. The fire was discovered about 11:30 at night in the store owned by Louis Lerner. A strong wind was blowing north, and the fire quickly spread to other buildings. It spread so rapidly that neither property nor merchandise could be saved. Since some of the stores were covered with iron and were liberally doused with water, such as John Pahl's furniture and hardware store, they did not catch fire. (Courtesy of the Sister Bay Historical Society.)

The present-day Door County Ice Cream Factory was built at the northern edge of Sister Bay in 1912 by Albin Mickelson and his brothers as a general store. Mickelson had a store in the central part of the village a few years earlier that burned down. From the earliest days of the factory, ice cream and Mickelson's root beer, which he personally made, sold well. Some of the original planks used when the store was built are still in the store today. A few years after the original store was built, the addition (above) and a kitchen were added in the rear. (Courtesy of the Blossom Family Archives.)

The above photo was taken in 1904. The boats *Leona R.* and *Hustler* were owned by Adolph Roeser. Although there appear to be plenty of passengers on what probably was a Sunday afternoon, the boats were usually utilized to haul produce to Sister Bay. Notice the huge mounds of cordwood in the background—probably several hundred tons—which was still a huge resource for providing heat. (Courtesy of the Robert Berns Collections.)

Laughing Water was a fishing boat owned and operated around 1910 by Herman Erickson, who worked for C.R. Seaquist, a fish dealer. Herring fishing was a big business in the Sister Bay area at that time. The fish would be immediately dressed and prepared for shipment to distances as far as Chicago and other Midwestern cities. In the spring, the fish were salted, and in winter, they were iced. (Courtesy of Helen Carlson.)

Although *Sailor Boy* (above) took hundreds of local residents, vacationers, and visitors to numerous points around Green Bay from as far north as Detroit Island to Marinette, Ephraim, and Fish Creek, it probably did a bigger business with the products it had in storage. It brought cloth, apples, potatoes, and farm implements, and usually accepted in exchange eggs, butter, hides, and home-canned fruits. Barter was the more accepted form of exchange. Few cash transactions were made. (Courtesy of the Kathy Ray Collection.)

The Roeser dock in early Sister Bay was usually a hub of activity. Each of the three boats pictured above may have been delivering a different product to Sister Bay on the same day. Since horses were quite scarce in early Sister Bay, and boats were quite plentiful, people would take a Sunday ride on a boat just for pleasure. The price was right—a trip from Sister Bay to Ephraim cost 10¢. (Courtesy of the Sister Bay Historical Society.)

An ore boat unloading at the Roeser dock in Sister Bay is pictured above around 1927. The shipment was probably coal, since coal furnaces were in use throughout the area. There is also a mound of stone on the dock indicating that much of the construction now utilized masonry. The feed mill is on the left.

Martin and Mary Jischke were part of the group shown above at the dock of Everett B. Clarke Company, probably during an early spring Sunday morning around 1910. They are waiting for a boat to come with seeds for the spring planting. Most boats came from Menomimee, which was the stop before arriving in Sister Bay. Clarke advertised his company as "seedsmen" who operated out of Millford, Connecticut. (Courtesy of George Jischke.)

Pictured above is Dr. Fickner's "Forest Ideal" retirement home in Sister Bay in the early years of the twentieth century. The building was later used as a restaurant and a nursing home, managed by Mr. and Mrs. Irwin Bastian. The building occupied the area behind today's St. Rosalia Church and was near the bluff overlooking Green Bay. (Courtesy of Allen Erickson.)

The family of Andre Roeser is pictured at left. Roeser was an early prominent and influential citizen in the establishment of Sister Bay. He was involved in several businesses and was said to have been a very "hard-driving man" who "ruled with an iron fist." A contemporary wrote, "Andre Roeser had enormous strength and could lift a 300-pound barrel of salt and never damp a brow." Andre is seated on the right, and his wife Leone is seated in the center. She was on constant call as a midwife. Others pictured are Matt (seated left) and standing (left to right): Emil, Margaret, Anna, Magdelena, and Adolph. The Roesers had nine children, two of which drowned off their own dock. (Courtesy of the Robert Berns Collections.)

This is a portrait of the Berns family in the early twentieth century. Standing, second from right, is Julia Berns, who was born in 1888 and married Adolph Roeser, who ran the lumber company in Sister Bay from 1912 to 1941. His business was originally established in 1878 and is believed to have been the earliest established in Sister Bay. Others standing in photo are (left to right): William, Isabelle, Anthony, Julia, and Edward; (seated, left to right) Clarence, Matt, Irving, Anna, and Elmer. (Courtesy of the Robert Berns Collections.)

Mrs. Wenzel Bunda, owner of Bunda's general store for many years, and her children, Leona, Mary, Anne, and Bill are pictured above. Leona married William Berns, who returned from World War I and set up his barber shop in the building that is now the Village View Motel. Mary married Martin Jischke who was postmaster of Sister Bay. Annie married Elmer Highlander, a dairy farmer who had house-to-house milk service, and Bill, who remained in retail sales with a drug store, married Alma Witalson. (Courtesy of the Kathy Ray Collection.)

The wedding photo of Mary (Worachek) Bunda and Wenzel Bunda was taken in Kewanee, Wisconsin, where they were married in 1885. Wenzel's health did not permit him to be an active farmer, so he came with Mary to Sister Bay and opened up a general store in 1888. Mary was an active seamstress who did a lot of sewing—including her own wedding gown. (Courtesy of George Jischke.)

John and Emma Pahl were very active on the social scene in early Sister Bay. They attended dances regularly as one author wrote, and "were regular patrons of Henry Pleck's dance hall where they waltzed, two-stepped, and fox trotted until the wee hours." Even though Emma "stood most of her 16-hour day, she just couldn't keep those neat, little buttoned shoes still." The Pahls also regularly went to Ellison Bay for dances. Sometimes the horses bogged down in the winter snow, so John and his friends would have to push the rig back to Sister Bay or carry the girls back.

John was responsible for the first schoolhouse in Sister Bay and served as the school clerk for many years. He belonged to the Sister Bay Men's Club and was active in the Chamber of Commerce. (Courtesy of the Kathy Ray Collection.)

Mrs. Wenzel Bunda, who operated the Sister Bay Post Office from her retail store, was also the postmaster of Sister Bay for many years. She is shown above, fourth from the left, in the bottom row, entertaining other postmasters from Wisconsin who were meeting in Sister Bay. (Courtesy of the Robert Berns Collections.)

Three

Economic Growth

Al Mickelson's general store at the north end of Sister Bay was purchased by Floyd Rhode, who installed gasoline pumps and, according to his advertising, carried "a complete line of groceries and meats" in the early 1960s when the above photo was taken. Rhode sold the business to Elaine and Greta Johns, who sold it to Kent and Bernice Czarnecki, who sold it to Paul and Evelyn Hulbert in 1976. Due to environmental concerns, the Hulberts took out the pumps in front of the store during their ten-year tenure at the store. They sold it to Doug and Pam Coulter. The store was idle for a few years in the early 1990s before it was purchased by its current owner, Jay Blossom. (Courtesy of the Sister Bay Historical Society.)

Martin Jischke's meat market, the Maple Inn, is pictured here in 1936. There was another meat market in the village located on the northern end. As one observer said, "the Catholics shopped at one, the Baptists at the other." Jischke kept his meat market until World War II. He closed it during the war, since he did not want to "keep up with the rationing." (Courtesy of George Jischke.)

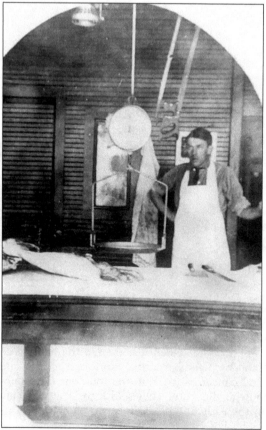

Martin Jischke is at work in his butcher shop at the north end of Sister Bay in the 1940s. The photo was taken to let everyone know that the shop just got a new scale.

Meat sold at the shop was purchased from the farmers and slaughtered in a house in the rear of the shop. When Jischke would slaughter beef, the owner would let him keep the hide. "If we were really lucky," says Jischke, "the hide would be worth about two dollars."

Jischke said he worked with a man who "could tell almost exactly how much meat there would be dressed out" just by looking at the live animal. Farmers would get the man's assessment before they would decide to slaughter the cattle for beef.

There was a problem that Jischke never could quite handle. After the cattle were slaughtered, the beef was treated with salt. On his deliveries to Emphrain and Ellison Bay, the salt would slowly drain from the beef. Twice his truck's bottom fell out, since the salt ate through the metal. "You know we didn't have plastic then," says Jischke, "and nothing we did kept the salt from getting to the bottom of the truck." (Courtesy of George Jischke.).

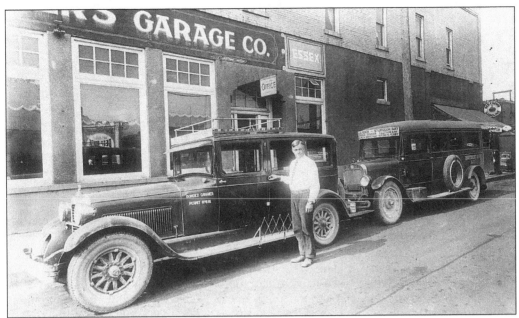

The first bus service for Door County was provided by Ernest Isaacson of Sister Bay. Shown above is the first bus of Isaacson's Northern Bus Line, which operated from Gill's Rock, the furthest northern village on the Door peninsula, to Sturgeon Bay where it met trains coming to the northernmost point in Door County. The first bus service was provided June 15, 1927, in a 1927 Hudson sedan with room for seven passengers. Service was provided to Gibralter schools starting in 1933. The bus line operated 12 months a year, and continued in operation until February 23, 1960. (Courtesy of Paul Hulbert.)

The Roen Steamship Company delivered coal to Sister Bay between 1941 and 1947. In the above photo, the Roen ship delivering 3,000 tons of coal is towed into Sister Bay by the barge, *Hilda*. The coal was picked up in Toledo, taken around Michigan by water, and delivered to Sister Bay. Later, shipments of coal arrived by truck. Four different kinds of coal were used in Sister Bay, with hardly any soft coal in use at any time. (Courtesy of the Robert Berns Collections.)

Clarence Brodd built a garage and service station in Sister Bay in 1928. Gasoline was sold using the "gravity system." Large glass containers held the gasoline—usually 20 gallons—above the pump. A customer would purchase as much gasoline as desired by watching it drain from the tank into the automobile. The customer would stop at a line that would indicate how many gallons remained in the glass container, and the owner would calculate how much gasoline was taken. Today this site is Johnny G's. (Courtesy of the Sister Bay Historical Society.)

During the early 1930s, Clarence Brodd had a service station on the corner of today's Highway 42 and Route ZZ. He purchased the site from Elmer and Lawrence Husby, who had a farm machine shop. Brodd was also a sub-dealer selling Chevrolets for the Felhofer brothers of Valmy. Clarence had a garage that he rented from Emil Becker from 1923 to 1924. He then built a garage at the site of what is now Johnny G's before moving to the above location. (Courtesy of the Robert Berns Collections.)

Sister Bay Motors and the Ford dealership in Sister Bay are pictured here as they looked in the 1950s. Ernest Isaacson built the original garage, which was known as Sister Bay Auto in 1919. He had a Ford dealership at the same site. At the time there were only ten automobiles in Liberty Grove Township and Sister Bay, an area that is approximately one-sixth of the entire Door County. After six years, Isaacson sold Sister Bay Auto to Leonard Swenson. Isaacson had a Model T Ford he used in 1924 to build the first snowmobile in Door County. That snowmobile was used to transport people to the hospital in emergency situations. It easily made the trip across Green Bay to Marinette and made 13 trips to Sturgeon Bay during its first winter in use. (Courtesy of the Sister Bay Historical Society.)

Joe Hendrickson's Texaco Garage and Service Station in Sister Bay is shown here as it looked around 1960. Hendrickson was a "well-known automobile doctor," as some Sister Bay residents still recall. With his partner, Tony Koessel, they serviced and repaired many autos in Sister Bay. Today, Hendrickson's former business site is a public park. (Courtesy of the Sister Bay Historical Society.)

51

Leonard Swenson, who had been active in the automobile business in Sister Bay since he sold two Model T Fords in 1927, purchased the Shell Service Station from Otto Fandret several years later. The property is located a few doors north of the intersection of Highway 42 and Route ZZ. Today, the building on the right in the above photo is an ice cream shop, and the garage on the left is used to paint signs. (Courtesy of the Sister Bay Historical Society.)

Around 1960, the Cities Service station at the northern end of the Village of Sister Bay was owned by L.C. Logerquist. It then became the B&F Citgo Service Station, a Union 76 Service Station, and has been Bhirdo's Shell Service Station since 1998. (Courtesy of the Sister Bay Historical Society.)

During World War II, the Berns Brothers Lumber Company of Sister Bay harvested trees on Chambers Island for use in their business. After logs were cut, usually in 12 or 20-foot lengths (although the length of the logs in the above photo is 16 feet), they were hauled on horse-drawn sleds to the beach area. Skidways had to be built to move logs from a higher point to the sled. One horse would be used to pull the log through the woods to a skidway. At times, loading jammers were used to lift logs on to the sleds. This means of transporting logs was an established practice between December and March. (Courtesy of the Robert Berns Collections.)

Warren Weigand and Willard Sunstrom (on the left) of Berns Brothers Lumber Company in Sister Bay prepare a shipment of logs from Chambers Island to the company. The truck of "Mac" McDonald from Michigan is being used since Berns Brothers did not have a skidway in the area, and there was a considerable distance to the beach. Notice the pipes in the rear of the truck. They could be extended so the truck could haul 20-foot logs. (Courtesy of the Robert Berns Collections.)

Logs on Chambers Island await transport to the Berns Brother Lumber Company in Sister Bay. They are stacked on the beach in piles that are about 10 feet high and about 50 to 60 feet deep. There were anywhere from 10 to 15 skidways at any one time, each with about 400 to 500 logs, waiting to cross Green Bay to go to the mill at Berns Brothers Lumber Company. (Courtesy of the Robert Berns Collections.)

Two skids would be emptied into a boom to make the 11-mile trip from Chambers Island to the Berns Brothers Lumber Company in Sister Bay. Softwoods such as hemlock, pine, and white poplar were transported this way since they float. The boom would travel about 1 mile an hour, so the trip took 10 to 11 hours. Attempts to move faster would cause the logs to pop out, and the bay had to be calm as well. Two men usually followed in a rowboat behind the boom to retrieve any logs that would pop out. When an unexpected storm would develop, as many as one hundred logs could be lost, later to be found washed ashore as far as Ellison Bay, about four miles north of Sister Bay. (Courtesy of the Robert Berns Collections.)

Hardwoods such as birch, maple, and oak could not float, so they were sawed on Chambers Island and shipped above water. This photo shows a shipment of oak logs that were sawed on Chambers Island, then hauled to Oconto and unloaded at Holt Hardwood Company. They were made into oak flooring that was delivered to Milwaukee, where the Berns Brothers Lumber Company had an agent who sold the finished product to large construction companies. Berns Brothers had a campsite on Lost Lake on Chambers Island. Provisions were available here for eight men to sleep overnight, with one being a cook. The work shift started Monday morning when they arrived, and lasted until Friday evening when they left the island and returned to Sister Bay. (Courtesy of the Robert Berns Collections.)

During World War II, Berns Brothers Lumber Company could not purchase wood from the west or south, since that wood was needed by the U.S. government for the war effort. Other arrangements had to be made. The Sister Bay lumber company purchased 440 acres on Chambers Island, a short distance from the village, and a U.S. forest ranger would mark trees ready for harvesting. Chambers Island was heavily wooded, so there was little concern that the island would be cut bare. The hemlock log pictured at right, which measured 48 inches in diameter, was harvested at Chambers Island and is shown being delivered to Berns Brothers Lumber in Sister Bay. Robert Berns, one of the owners of the company, states that the wood from Chambers Island was the "best lumber we ever used." (Courtesy of the Robert Berns Collections.)

The old indoor sawmill built by Adolph Roeser was still in use for many years by Berns Brothers Lumber of Sister Bay. The first mill, constructed on the same site, was built by Andre Roeser, Adolph's father, in 1877. It burned to the ground in 1887, and was rebuilt by Andre, only to burn down again in 1907. When the above mill was built, a four-story flourmill was also constructed within 100 feet of the sawmill. That flourmill burned down in the 1930s. In the above photo, perhaps taken in the 1960s, Jack Stadler (on the right), the mill foreman, directs Roy Graf (extreme left) and Eric Anderson (center, in the background) as a log (upper center background) is being sawed into two pieces of lumber, each 2 inches by 8 inches. (Courtesy of the Robert Berns Collections.)

The Berns Brothers Lumber Company millwork and carpenter shop in Sister Bay is pictured above. Windows, window frames, doors, and cherry ladders were the principal items made in the shop, which operated 12 months a year with a minimum of four employees. Shown above are Arnold Foxworthy and Everette Johnson, the shop foreman. Foxworthy was a local builder who, like others, would come in to work on custom jobs. The biggest project completed in the shop required 1.5 million feet of lumber. It was a contract with the U.S. government to build a crate to be used for a searchlight unit in the Soviet Union after World War II. (Courtesy of the Sister Bay Historical Society.)

This photo depicts a meeting of possible sales representatives at the Barker Lumber and Fuel Company of Sister Bay in the 1920s. The site, which included a feed mill, was south of the Wiltse dock, which is now Anchor Sam's. Most of the lumber sold was for use with finished products and for other needs in the interior of buildings. The business was bought out by Berns Brothers in the early 1940s. (Courtesy of Helen Carlson.)

The Berns Brothers Lumber Company office was located near the original Roeser dock at Mill Road and Maple Drive. John Holland, the architect, and Robert Berns, one of the owners of the company, accepted an architectural award for the design of the building, presented by the Small Business Association at McCormick Place in Chicago in 1947. The award cited exceptional use of the design of the cathedral ceiling in the building. (Courtesy of the Sister Bay Historical Society.)

The Jungwirth hardware store was opened in 1948–49 at the intersection of Highway 42 and Route ZZ. Since that time, it has remained in the Jungwirth family. Joseph and Winnie Jungwirth sold the store to David and Priscilla Jungwirth in 1976. The Ace affiliation began in 1953. A new roof was built in 1976, replacing the pitched roof that was in existence at the time. The facade of the building was also considerably changed at the time. (Courtesy of the Sister Bay Historical Society.)

The Hagedorn Studio opened for business in Sister Bay around 1960. Subsequently, it became a Cove Gift Shop, then Fan-Tastic Sports, and today it is Bareware Two. Bernie Hagedorn was a professional photographer and very active in community activities. He served as general chairman of the Golden Jubilee celebration and prepared photos of early Sister Bay, some of which have graciously been made available for publication in this book by the Sister Bay Historical Society. (Courtesy of the Sister Bay Historical Society.)

The above photo from the early 1960s depicts, above the main entrance, a sign for the Clover Farm Stores Hillside Market. The street sign reads Herman's Markets, as does the sign on the side of the building. To most residents in Sister Bay at this time, it was known as Herman's Hillside. Previously it had been Clarence Brodd's garage, a furniture store, and Peterson's Restaurant. In 1972, it became Woerfel's Deli, then the Door Deli in 1981, the Village Deli and Market in 1999, and Johnny G's in 2000. (Courtesy of the Sister Bay Historical Society.)

Elmer Berns built a feed mill near Roeser's Dock, which he sold in January 1952. The building reopened as the Door County Cooperative with Kenneth Larson and Albert Prost in charge. Feed, seed, and fertilizers were sold, and custom grinding was available. Most of the farmers in Door County belonged to the Co-op. (Courtesy of the Sister Bay Historical Society.)

F.V. Hedeen, shown in this photo taken in the 1930s, would often haul cherries from his Crescent Orchards in Sister Bay to Chicago, where he sold them at the fresh produce markets. Hedeen made weekly trips from mid-July to mid-August. Other fruit growers would take their produce to the old Wiltse's dock, which became known as the produce dock and then Anchor Sam's. Much of the fruit was also canned and later frozen. There was a Farm Growers Co-op that did its canning in a factory on Route ZZ and Olde Stage Road, just east of Sister Bay. Some local growers also provided produce processed by Reynolds Brothers from Sturgeon Bay. (Courtesy of Jo Ann Thomas.)

Clemens Hedeen and Hjalmar Seaquist take a moment's rest in their cherry orchards near Sister Bay. The 120-acre property on today's Hill Road was located approximately 1 mile from the village. Eventually they purchased additional acreage near what is now Hillcrest and Water's End Roads and had cherry production from 10,000 trees in their orchards. Harvesting the crop required a vast amount, and a great variety of, workers, including teenage boys from Chicago, employees from the Ford plant in Iron Mountain, Michigan, when it closed for re-tooling, Oneida Indians, Texans, Mexicans, Boy Scouts, Jamaicans, Mexican nationals, and migrants from Barbados. (Courtesy of Jo Ann Thomas.)

For more than a century, soil throughout Door County proved conducive to the growth of various types of fruit. Since cherries quickly thrived in the area, orchards sprang up throughout the county. Picking the fruit turned out to be a burdensome chore. Thousands of workers—some estimates range as high as 15,000 for one harvest season—were imported, including migrants, prisoners of war, and children. They would work from sunrise to sunset, filling as many 9-pound buckets of cherries as quickly as possible, and earning about 25¢ per bucket.

Dale Seaquist of the Seaquist Orchards in Sister Bay closely studied machines that were being developed in order to shake cherries from the tree into large boxes. These "shakers" shook individual branches and often would damage the tree. A refinement of this method evolved, and "trunk shakers" were employed. This required workers to lift boxes and move them to large tanks. Seaquist developed a catching device that eliminated much of the manual labor. A further development was a machine known as a "one-man harvester," which is shown above. It would fold around the bottom of a tree and open into a large upside-down shaped umbrella. The machine pictured above has been in use since the 1980s. (Courtesy of the *Door Reminder*.)

Once a mechanical picker is in position, it shakes the cherries from the tree. A human picking cherries would be able to pick about 500 pounds on an average day. The mechanical picker could "pick" (or shake off) the same amount of cherries in about two minutes. Dale Seaquist's refinements of earlier mechanical pickers had cherries falling from trees onto a conveyor belt, operated as a separate machine, directly to the processing plant. (Courtesy of the *Door Reminder*.)

61

When cherries arrive at the processing plant, they are poured into a large vat like the one in the above photo. Small cherries are removed, all cherries are stripped of stems, and an electronic eye is able to detect bruised cherries, which are then discarded. Pictured above is Ray Torres of the Seaquist Orchards in Sister Bay, maintaining an orderly flow of cherries to the conveyor belt. (Courtesy of the *Door Reminder*.)

A conveyor belt at the processing plant owned by the Seaquist Orchards takes selected cherries to be pitted by 11 pitting machines, which pitted 4.5 million pounds of cherries in 1999—approximately 55 percent of the total cherry production in the state of Wisconsin. Approximately 40 percent of that total was grown on the 700 acres of the Seaquist Orchards, located immediately north of the Village of Sister Bay. (Courtesy of the *Door Reminder*.)

Inconcio Sugura of the Seaquist Orchards makes a final inspection of the cherries at the processing plant. They are then shipped frozen in 30-pound packages and are used mainly for pies and cooking. In recent years, large markets have developed for dried cherries and cherry juice, which is used to blend with other fruit juices. (Courtesy of the *Door Reminder*.)

The structure pictured at right appears to be a silo. It is located in the middle of a field just off Hill Road at the north end of Sister Bay. It was painted in 1999 to depict the Danish national flag. The owner of the property on which the "silo" stands claims that he investigated the floor design to "check out" if the structure could have been used as a guard tower to watch over German prisoners of war sent to the area to pick cherries toward the end of World War II. He states that the guard towers had similar floor plans, but others who lived in the area at the time insist that this structure was never used as a guard tower. Still others believe that the building may have been occupied at the time the German prisoners of war were in Door County, giving it the appearance that they were guards, however unlikely a German escape attempt was.

Pictured above is a converted Model T ice machine used for sawing ice in and around Sister Bay, at Europe Lake and Baileys Harbor between 1941 and 1947. It had a hand-built gas-driven engine, with blades of 36 or 40 inches. The cut ice would be stored locally by fishermen. Resorts would also put ice into their own icehouses for use during the summer season. Berns Brothers Lumber Company also stored ice to sell and deliver throughout the county during the summer months. (Courtesy of the Robert Berns Collections.)

Channels such as the one shown at left were used when harvesting cakes of ice in Sister Bay. Workers in the background would saw the ice by hand into cakes to feed the channel. The ice cakes would be pushed along the channel until they arrived at a gas-driven elevator that would lift them onto the trucks to be hauled away. (Courtesy of the Robert Berns Collections.)

A long channel was necessary to deliver the ice that had been sawed into cakes from Green Bay to the waiting trucks about 70 to 80 feet away from the ice field. Although the ice would be 12 inches or thicker, trucks were not parked on the ice when they were loaded with the ice cakes. Depending on the thickness of the ice, as many as 3,000 cakes were cut and hauled away in a single day. (Courtesy of the Robert Berns Collections.)

Two trucks are pictured above being loaded with cakes of ice cut from Sister Bay. Sometimes as many as eight trucks were loading at the same time when the ice was being harvested. The ice cakes ranged in weight from 100 to 200 pounds, depending on the thickness of the ice, which ranged from 14 to 23 inches. Each truck carried from two to four tons in one load. (Courtesy of the Robert Berns Collections.)

George Jischke, son of Martin and Mary Jischke, shows off his Sunday best in front of the home his parents built in Sister Bay in 1920. It was one of the first homes in the village to have gas lighting. The building also housed the village post office, which was mainly a large room, 22 feet by 26 feet. The room stored the many catalog items ordered by people in the village and the luggage usually sent ahead by visitors planning to spend the summer in Sister Bay. It was also not uncommon for live animals, mostly chickens, to be sent through the mail at that time. The Jischkes ran the post office in Sister Bay until 1934. (Courtesy of George Jischke.)

The former Liberty Grove Town Hall, located at the northern end of the Village of Sister Bay, is currently a retail establishment called Ecology Sportswear. It has served numerous purposes since it was built, probably near the turn of the century. Liberty Grove elections were conducted there, as were township meetings. The two major issues considered were care of the roads in the township and snow removal. There were also numerous church activities held at the hall, particularly those associated with the Moravian church. Area schools—Wildwood and those from Ellison Bay—put on theater productions and Christmas pageants in the hall. The most important use of the town hall occurred in 1918, when the health commissioner closed schools, churches, and most public places because of a flu epidemic. All necessary activities for the area were conducted from the town hall.

The Nor-Door Clinic in Sister Bay was made possible after a local group of residents formed the Nor-Door Medical Board. Sam Subin was elected president, and the group was able to recruit Dr. E.C. Farmer from Washington Island in 1957. Dr. Farmer set up his office in the former residence of Martin Jischke. A fund drive was launched, and necessary funds were raised to formally dedicate the clinic in September 1960. The clinic was located south of Clyde Casperson's Funeral Home. Al Johnson eventually bought it out as he expanded his restaurant facilities. (Courtesy of the Sister Bay Historical Society.)

The Sister Bay community hall and library were opened in 1941. A local newspaper account stated, "The community hall and public library [are] an imposing structure for a community this size." The structure was 76 feet by 40 feet, with an "L" 20 feet by 20 feet for the public library. The auditorium has a seating capacity of three hundred. Funds for the building were provided by a $6,000 bond issue, with an additional $4,000 added at a later date. Much of the labor for the project was furnished by the National Youth Administration. The library was assigned to J.C.M. Hanson, former chief of the Library of Congress, who retired to Sister Bay and had established a permanent residence there.

The Bunda general store in Sister Bay, located at the corner of Highway 42 and Route ZZ, burned to the ground June 25, 1942. The store was the largest store in Door County north of Sturgeon Bay at the time. Owner William Bunda estimated the loss at between $80,000 and $100,000. The store had been recently remodeled, and a grand opening was set for the day after the fire. A Bunda store on the same site had been destroyed by fire 30 years earlier. Bunda built a third store on the same site and opened it as a Rexall Drug Store. (Courtesy of Helen Carlson.)

William Bunda Sr. opened the Bunda Rexall Drug Store in 1945, at the same location where the general store of Mrs. W. Bunda stood for many years on the corner of Highway 42 and Route ZZ, at the southern edge of the business district of Sister Bay. The store also sold clothing and household implements. Bunda moved his business to the Sister Bay Mall, on the top of the hill in the southern section of the village. The site pictured above has been vacant or partially occupied for limited periods in recent years. However, it is scheduled to open as Sister Bay's Village Exchange in 2000. (Courtesy of the Sister Bay Historical Society.)

This is the Masterfreeze Corporation building as it appeared in 1945. In earlier years, Emil Becker built the first garage of Sister Bay on this site and until World War II, Algeron Smith operated it as a body shop. Later, additions increased floor space at Masterfreeze to 27,000 feet. Pre-fab walk-in coolers and freezers were manufactured. In 1958, Armstrong Cork Company signed an exclusive franchise to distribute Masterfreeze products. Production stopped at the plant in 1960–61, and the building was empty for several years. Since 1978, the Walkway shops have occupied the location that formerly had been the Masterfreeze Corporation. (Courtesy of the Sister Bay Historical Society.)

The Cozy Nook Beauty Shop is pictured above as it appeared in the mid-1960s, when it was owned by Georgia Staver, who retired. It was then owned by Kurt Lindum and in 1994, after a room was added to the back, it became Freshwater Gifts owned by Sue Woerful, who also owns Johnny G's located one door south. (Courtesy of the Sister Bay Historical Society.)

Anchor Sam's Yacht Harbor, the former Wiltse dock and the former produce dock, opened for business in 1956. Sam Subin came to Door County in the early 1940s. He quickly found Door County to his liking and looked around for a place he could start a boat yard. According to a newspaper account, "Sam's objective was to have a one-stop service for touring yachtsmen, where they could get supplies, needed repairs, gasoline, water, and be able to fill their galleys with everything from baked beans to fine pastry." For those who wanted to stay, dockage, storage, and complete service were also available. The business has maintained these goals until the present time. (Courtesy of the Sister Bay Historical Society.)

In 1949, Joseph Dlouhy came to Sister Bay from Chicago to retire. He had been visiting his summer home in the area for years. Dlouhy, who had been a businessman in Chicago, quickly discovered that he was not ready to retire. He opened Salty Joe's in the middle of Sister Bay in a building that had been built for a post office decades before. Dlouhy's approach to advertising was somewhat unorthodox. His ads would announce "Try Our Tasteless Cocktail Shrimp and Puny Lobster Tails," or "You Can Take Home Some of Our Questionable Cheese, Too, in Your Favorite Gift Wrapping—Newspapers." He also warned potential customers, "Opened Fish Parlor Way Back in '49—Still Have Some of the Original Fish."

Windows in his store would advertise "Stinky, Smelly, Slimy Fish." After someone would enter the store, they might see a sign—"Fish are like Relations: After four days they stink." When buying a newspaper from the stand in front of his store, customers were warned, "these papers are not for sale." Customers were also cautioned because all the newspapers were old, and when someone complained about this, Dlouhy would say that he warned people not to buy them and pointed to the sign. Nevertheless, many customers filled the coin box. They also contributed $75 to a jar labeled "Salty Joe's Florida Vacation Fund." The money was used to help purchase an intercom system at the local high school.

According to almost all his customers, Dlouhy had a successful business. As a newspaper reported, "[h]is customers have learned that behind the insults is a man who is both good-hearted and honest, a man who is aware of the value of both his merchandise and his friends, a man who is acquainted with the foibles of human nature, but is determined to laugh at them and not deny them."

After Dlouhy died June 7, 1969, the site reopened as the Elbow Room. After that, it operated as D'Amico's Pizza for 11 years, before changing owners and opening in 1999 as Dano's Pizza. In 2000, the name was changed to Trattoria. (Courtesy of the Sister Bay Historical Society.)

SALTY JOE'S PERSONAL GUARANTEE TO YOU

I, Salty Joe, do hereby personally and unequivocally guarantee that the enclosed badly-packaged and ill-smelling so-called ''gift'' items, which are being sent to you at the behest and insistence of your questionable friend (s) _____, are not fit for human consumption, and will undoubtedly cause acute indigestion, backache, severe heart-burn, inertia, laryngitis, colon spasms, athlete's foot, and, in some cases, total collapse.

No care has been taken to insure the palatibility of these indigestible delicacies, and you are strictly on your own if you insist upon partaking of any or all of these beaten-up foods so carefully and gleefully selected by your above mentioned friend (s).

However, if, through some fault of my own, I have failed to deliver this package to you in a thoroughly dessicated or rancid condition, I shall hold myself fully responsible for this oversight; and I do hereby agree that if, at the present time, you are at least seventy-five years of age and in poor health, and will present this certificate to me personally fifty years from the date of its issuance, at any of my offices (the exact location of said offices to be announced later), I shall personally replace this package at absolutely no cost to yourself, with one that is all that I have claimed it to be.

S-o-o-o-o-o-o-o-O-O- eat everything in good health - - - - - the bad health will follow ! !
And I am adding the following so that you WILL feel that you are fully protected:

COUNTY OF   <u>Whatsis</u>   )
STATE OF   <u>Confusion</u>) ss.

SALTY JOE, appearing before me this blankety blank day of blank, deposes and says that he is the ''Salty'' salt mentioned in this guarantee and that as far as he is aware, the foods he dispenses are every bit as old as claimed, and in some cases are definitely MUCH older !

SALTY JOE further deposes and says that tests have been made at various times of the aforesaid products, but that no person is now living to prove how thoroughly accurate they were. However, if you will contact the relatives of these unfortunate persons (of which ''Salty'' has a long list), they will undoubtedly confirm the absolute success of the tests.

_____
The ''Salty'' salt

Signed and attested to before me this blankety blank day of blank, of this blankety blank year.

_____
U. R. NEXT - - LOCO ATTORNEY

Why customers felt compelled to get this type of "personal guarantee" when purchasing something from Salty Joe's Fish Shop in Sister Bay could perhaps explain the store's success. (Courtesy of Helen Carlson.)

The Sister Bay I.G.A. (Independent Grocers Association) store was owned by the Orin Hanson family. It was sold to Jack Manson, who sold it to Clyde Brown, who had ideas for opening a restaurant. Those plans did not materialize, and it was sold to Axel (Al) Albert Johnson and his two partners in 1948. It was turned into Al Johnson's Swedish Restaurant and was open to the public in 1949, with 60 seats. (Courtesy of the Al Johnson Family Archives.)

Al Johnson's has undergone several changes since 1949, including insulating the building, until the above major remodeling was completed. The restaurant maintained this basic outside design until 1973. With the temperature below freezing for most of the winter, and Al Johnson attending training for the FBI, the restaurant kept sporadic hours at this time. However, with the increased traffic to Sister Bay, the restaurant has operated continuously on a daily basis since the mid-1960s. (Courtesy of the Sister Bay Historical Society.)

In 1973, additional grounds were added to the Al Johnson's Restaurant property to make room for a lobby and gift shop. The properties of Edith Lyle Carlson were purchased as was the Nor-Door Clinic. The former Lyle residence is now used as an office by Al Johnson after it was moved about 2,000 feet. Lyle also owned eight cottages that were moved about 100 feet and are now used for storage. Parking space was increased, and interior seating was expanded to accommodate 120 individuals. One of Sweden's major holidays is Midsummer Fest, and this is celebrated at Al Johnson's on Saturday, June 21, or the closest Saturday to that date. Uniforms are made especially for all employees at Al Johnson's to add to the festive atmosphere, which is maintained throughout the year. Johnson has been questioned several times about why he imported logs from Norway to make his Swedish restaurant authentic. With a grin and an exasperated shrug, he says he tried and tried, but the "red tape in Sweden was just unbelievable," so he settled for logs from Norway. (Courtesy of the Al Johnson Family Archives.)

Al Johnson received a strange, but as later events were to prove, a most ingenious gift for his birthday on December 9, 1972. Mitch "Wink" Larsen walked into the restaurant with a goat, properly decorated with ribbons on its horns, and presented it to Johnson. There was discussion about placing the goat on the roof. The restaurant sign had a small roof with a layer of sod added to experiment with keeping the sod alive on the entire roof. It was discovered that a finely-textured waffle vinyl-like plastic sheet about one quarter inch thick would prevent the dirt from sliding off and keep the moisture in place so the sod would not dry out, but prevent the moisture from seeping through the roof.

The above photo depicts Larsen a few seconds after he released Oscar, the first goat to roam the roof of Al Johnson's Restaurant. Through the years, as many as eight to ten goats could be seen on the roof. Depending on the weather, they can be observed from about 8:00 a.m. until 7:00 p.m., when they are taken to a farm a few miles away. (Courtesy of the Al Johnson Family Archives.)

Emma Husby was in the restaurant business in Sister Bay for many years. She earned about $3.00 a week in the 1930s, shortly after she opened her own restaurant, which she named Emma's Restaurant. Her duties included cooking breakfast, lunch, and dinner. Between meals, Emma made bakery goods and ice cream to be sold at the restaurant. A chicken plate cost 25¢. Even as late as the 1960s, when Emma was in a wheelchair, she continued to operate the restaurant. She would serve drinks from behind the bar in her wheelchair, in which she would often remain overnight at the restaurant. Emma died in 1974. (Courtesy of the Sister Bay Historical Society.)

Husby's, a restaurant in Sister Bay, is located across the street from the current Sister Bay Bowl. At the turn of the century it was Louis Lerner's clothing store. Emma Husby bought the site from Frank Bunda in 1930 and opened it as Emma's Restaurant, even though there was no running water or electricity. A few years later, the restaurant's name was changed to the Cherryland Restaurant. (Courtesy of the Sister Bay Historical Society.)

74

The above photo depicts a major addition to the former Cottage Restaurant, which is now the Sister Bay Cafe. The addition was made in 1960 and increased seating capacity from 35 to 55. A few years later, another addition was added and used as a storage and prep room. A blacksmith shop occupied the site before World War II, when it was purchased by Hans Hensen. He then built a private residence. It was remodeled as a restaurant by Charlie Porier in 1939–40 and opened as the Cottage Restaurant. The sign for the restaurant was purchased at the 1933 World's Fair in Chicago. Clara and Alonso Englesby purchased the property in 1945 and sold it to John Vieth in 1946 for $9,000. Vieth sold the property in 1987, and it remained the Cottage Restaurant. The *Milwaukee Journal* featured the restaurant and several of its recipes for bread pudding and pancakes in the September 9, 1982, food section. David Daubner purchased the restaurant in 1994 and changed the name to the Sister Bay Cafe. (Courtesy of the Sister Bay Historical Society.)

A "typical" Door County snowstorm in 1978 ended up covering the Cottage Restaurant. It only snowed about 3 feet, but the drifts, as is common, were over 20 feet—enough to completely cover the restaurant. John Beckstrom, pictured above, uncovered a corner of the roof of the restaurant so this photo could be taken. He is probably about 10 to 12 feet above ground level. The owner was happy to find no major damage. (Courtesy of John Vieth.)

The former St. Rosalia's Church of Sister Bay, built in the early 1900s, was purchased by Gary and Mary Ann Guterman in 1984. It was opened as the Mission Grille in 1989, with a 1950s motif. There was a soda fountain, jukeboxes, four billiard tables, a 1940 Heritage Classic Harley Davidson motorcycle, an arcade game, an old Coca-Cola clock, and many tin signs of the period along with original movie posters. This basic theme for the restaurant was kept intact until 1993. (Courtesy of the Guterman Family.)

In 1991, the Mission Grille—the former St. Rosalia's Church of Sister Bay—added a patio and expanded the kitchen to three times its former size. New stained glass windows portraying a religious theme were incorporated into the design of the building. The original church did not have any stained glass windows. In the above photo from 1993, a front veranda was in place where meals could be served from May through October. The large 7-foot Trinity window was set in place, and in 1998 stained glass was added to the window. The veranda was enclosed that same year. In 1999, the restaurant was presented an award of excellence by *Wine Spectator* magazine for its wine list and menu. (Courtesy of the Guterman Family.)

During the 1950s, Pisha's Restaurant was owned by Roy and Irene Knudson. After it was sold, it became Keneavy Kitchen in 1978. Fifteen years later, it was sold again and is now known as the Inn at Kristofer's. A second level was added in 1995. The *Milwaukee Journal* named it one of the top one hundred restaurants in the State of Wisconsin in 1997. In 1999, the same newspaper also selected it as one of the five most romantic restaurants in the state. (Courtesy of the Sister Bay Historical Society.)

The Sister Bay Bowl is pictured above as it appeared around 1960. When league play was introduced here in November of 1958, the popularity of the sport skyrocketed. Automatic pin-spotters were installed in 1959 for the six lanes. The bowlers were out in full force seven nights a week. Men's teams occupied the lanes three nights a week, with six teams bowling a night. The women had 12 teams that bowled twice a week. The Door County Tavern League started in 1960, with the Sister Bay Bowl hosting the play, which took place for six weeks between April and May. Between 90 to 100 teams participated. There was also a contest to determine a "King of the Bowl," which was restricted to local residents. Although league play is not as active as it was throughout the 1960s and 1970s, the Sister Bay lanes still attract some league play and weekend bowling parties. (Courtesy of the Sister Bay Historical Society.)

Jake Kodanko had a fleet of trucks that were used throughout Door County. Many of them hauled stone from the Manson Pit Quarry near Sister Bay. The Manson Pit Quarry on North Bay Road about 4 miles east of Sister Bay was started in the 1940s, and operated until the early 1990s. The quarry produced much of the crushed stone that was used for highway development in Door County. Kodanko was a popular figure in Sister Bay and has been described as "one of Northern Door County's best-loved characters." Known as "Robbie," he loved a good joke—especially when it was on him. The Village of Sister Bay, and everyone who knew the 40-year-old bachelor, were stunned when he drowned in Green Bay in January 1963 when the truck he was driving went through the ice. (Courtesy of the Sister Bay Historical Society.)

The Zion Lutheran Church, built in 1887, was purchased by a private party in 1993. All pews, except for two, were removed. Of the eight stained glass windows, two were left for the new owners who found the original windows, refinished them, and placed them back in the church. The circle window visible at the front of the church and the peaked windows on the sides are all the original windows. The cross atop the church is believed to be the original cross in place since the time the church was built. The cross was removed in 1996. The building is now a commercial business, the Tannenbaum Holiday Shop. The church membership of the Zion Lutheran Church merged with another congregation in Ellison Bay in a new church building constructed for both congregations, Shepherd of the Bay. (Courtesy of the Tannenbaum Holiday Shop.)

The administration building for the Village of Sister Bay on Maple Street was built in the 1930s. For a few years, it was the Sister Bay station of the Bank of Sturgeon Bay, then it was the Baylake Bank, and it has been the administration building for the Village of Sister Bay since 1972. (Courtesy of the Sister Bay Historical Society.)

The Wilke Furniture store as it appeared in the early 1960s is pictured above. The first building on the site was that of Ole Erickson, who built a general store almost a century ago upon arriving in Sister Bay from Washington Island with his wife, Rebecca. Stories are still told about how Erickson would meet the Goodrich boats arriving in Sister Bay with a wheelbarrow that he would load up with merchandise he would sell at the store. In 1936, the property was sold to Mrs. Gust Carlson who operated a restaurant on the site. After a few years, Carl Benson bought the building and turned it into a furniture store. John and Lucy Witalison then bought it in 1950 and continued to operate it as a furniture store. In 1960, Richard and Grace Wilke purchased the business and ran it until 1980, when they sold the property to Al and Ingret Johnson. The Wilkes continued working at the store which became, and remains, Al's Boutique on the Bay. (Courtesy of the Sister Bay Historical Society.)

The one hundred-year-old Koessel granary was moved in September 1998 from its farm location to a commercial site on the property of Domicile, an antique, craft, and art shop in Sister Bay. In the photo above, the granary is mounted on two steel I-beams, which run the length of the floor. These are connected to a third I-beam, making a "U" shape to balance the building as it is pulled. The building was moved 400 feet away to its new site. However, it had to travel more than 800 feet, since there was a lot of back and forth movement in attempting to keep the building flat for the entire trip. (Courtesy of Jane and John Kayser.)

Many businesses in Sister Bay are aware of preserving the historic past of Sister Bay and blending it with today's activities and economy. Domicile, an antique, craft, and art shop located on Highway 57 just south of the junction with Highway 42, purchased and moved a granary from the Koessel farm to its new location at Domicile. The granary is about one hundred years old and was in use until 1997. The current owners, Jane and John Kayser, will leave one of the shoots in place, and a bin will remain in one of the corners. There were two layers of barn board and two layers of floor. The porch(above) and new windows were added. The building is now officially known as "Stuff" and is used as a seasonal shop by Domicile.

Four

Religion

The Swedish Baptist Church of Sister Bay built the first church in the village, which was renovated and enlarged in 1902. A steeple, a tower, and a baptistery were added, and seating capacity was increased to three hundred. The basement was dug out so that a new furnace could be installed. The value of the church rose to $2,500. The church was free of debt when its 25th anniversary was celebrated. (Courtesy of the Archives of the First Baptist Church of Sister Bay.)

Rev. Charles Wassell is pictured here with his wife. Rev. Wassell became the first pastor of the Swedish Baptist Church when he accepted the call on September 5, 1881. Prior to that time, preachers visited the congregation for four years. Wassell was born in Sweden and immigrated to the United States. He responded to the invitation of the Swedish Baptist Church and came to visit the area. He slept in a hay barn in Rowleys Bay for several nights after accepting the call to be pastor, and soon purchased a farm near the area of today's Carroll House Restaurant in order to supplement his $200-a-year salary. (Courtesy of the Archives of the First Baptist Church of Sister Bay.)

Rev. Charles Palm, his wife (the former Anna Sophia Wassell, daughter of the first pastor of the Swedish Baptist Church in Sister Bay), and their daughter Agnes are pictured above. Rev. Palm was the pastor of the Bethel Baptist Church of Ellison Bay when it was organized in 1928, and he also assisted at the Swedish Baptist Church in Sister Bay. When Pastor C.B. Sanders resigned, Rev. Palm, then 80 years old, served as pastor for six months until a new pastor could be called. (Courtesy of the Archives of the First Baptist Church of Sister Bay.)

Some of the first charter members of the Swedish Baptist Church in Sister Bay included the George Johnson family, pictured at right in a family portrait. The Mission Circle of the church was organized in their home. The family moved to Humpherey Platte, Nebraska in 1881. (Courtesy of the Archives of the First Baptist Church of Sister Bay.)

The Newport Mission Church near Ellison Bay was built by the Swedish Baptist Church of Sister Bay in 1924. In 1890, there was a German Baptist Church at the site, but it had disbanded near the turn of the century. A settler from Sweden, John Carlson, purchased a farm adjacent to the church and secured permission from the American Baptist Home Mission to conduct Sunday School in the building. Baptist services began in the building in 1907. When the Newport Mission Church was organized, it had 36 charter members. Rev. Charles Palm was called to be the first pastor. The church property was transferred to the Bethel Baptist Church congregation in 1931. A clause in the deed stated that if the congregation should ever disband, the property would revert to the Swedish Baptist Church of Sister Bay. (Courtesy of the Archives of the First Baptist Church of Sister Bay.)

A major religious ceremony in the Swedish Baptist Church was confirmation for the young members of the congregation. Students attended classes for two or more years before their confirmation day. Pictured at left is Julia Carlson on her day of confirmation at the Swedish Baptist Church about 1900. (Courtesy of the Liberty Park Lodge.)

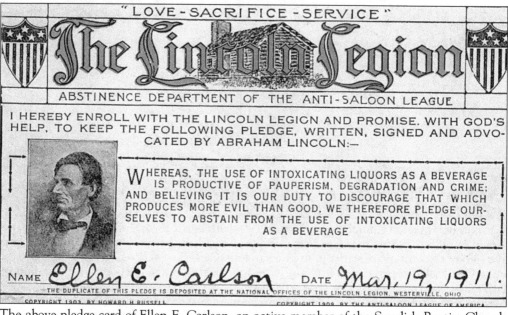

The above pledge card of Ellen E. Carlson, an active member of the Swedish Baptist Church of Sister Bay, was discovered in the church's archives along with other personal memorabilia reflecting the very active role of Carlson in church activities. (Courtesy of the Archives of the First Baptist Church of Sister Bay.)

Matilda and Mildred Anderson were married on the same day at the Swedish Baptist Church of Sister Bay. Pictured above (on the left) are: August Erickson, Matilda Anderson, and Beatrice Borg; (on the right) Carl Carlson, Mildred Anderson, and Margaret Seaquist. The date of the wedding was August 8, 1917. (Courtesy of the Archives of the First Baptist Church of Sister Bay.)

Groundbreaking for the new First Baptist Church of Sister Bay pictured above was October 13, 1974. The first services in the building were July 6, 1975, and dedication services later that year were held November 25–28. Land for the new church on Highway 42, the main road in Sister Bay, was donated in 1970 by Mr. and Mrs. Ragner Brogren.

After a successful three-year capital funds campaign, with the congregation committing itself to $74,000 for the new First Baptist Church of Sister Bay, a further decision was made to build a new sanctuary (shown above), a Christian education wing, and a fellowship hall. (Courtesy of the Archives of the First Baptist Church of Sister Bay.)

The first services of the Moravian Church of Sister Bay were held at the residence of Mr. and Mrs. Johnson in 1896. That building was remodeled for church services. Later that year, a log church, shown above, was purchased from the Free Baptists and became the regular church of the Moravian congregation in the Sister Bay area. (Courtesy of the Sister Bay Moravian Church Archives.)

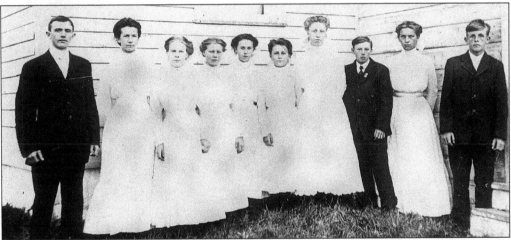

Members of the Moravian Church are prepared for confirmation by attending communicants' classes and demonstrating their understanding of Moravian church history, rituals, and traditions. Confirmation is a reconfirming of the candidate's baptismal faith and indicates the confirmed is ready to become an active member of the church. At the first confirmation of the Moravian Church of Sister Bay, nine individuals were accepted. The above photo depicts the 1908 confirmands. They are, from left to right: Jessie Christianson, Anna Evenson, Olga Jacobson, Amelia Larson, Violet Trucker, Edith Mickelson, Arnold Nelson, Mary Johnson, and Andy Husby. (Courtesy of the Sister Bay Moravian Church Archives.)

Youngsters attending the Sunday school of the Moravian Church of Sister Bay are pictured probably in the 1920s. At that time, the program was being conducted in the afternoons since the church was sharing a pastor with Ephraim, a condition which existed until 1946. One of the major projects of the Sunday school students was to prepare a Christmas pageant that would be viewed by the entire community. The Moravian Church in Sister Bay also had a strong camp program during this period, which was directed by May Charney. Students in seventh and higher grades attended the camp program. (Courtesy of the Sister Bay Moravian Church Archives.)

The Moravian Church of Sister Bay is pictured as it appears today. Numerous improvements have been made over the years since the church was closed in 1918 due to the influenza epidemic. A kitchen was added in 1928, and four stained glass windows were installed in 1929. A Sunday school room and a choir room were added 1955–58. In 1962, a new front entrance was dedicated—a few years after seating capacity was increased to 150. Rev. Jane Harberg, the current pastor of the Sister Bay Moravian Church of Sister Bay, was installed in 1992.

The Swedish Evangelical Lutheran Church, later called the Zion Lutheran Church, was organized July 13, 1978, when Pastor C.O. Olander conducted the first services for the congregation in a schoolhouse in Liberty Grove. A decision was made to follow the Augustana Synod, and preparations were made to build a church. Mr. and Mrs. P.W. Carlson deeded a half-acre of land on which the church would stand. On June 23, 1888, at a congregational meeting, a resolution was passed to call the church the Swedish Evangelical Lutheran Church. The church was dedicated August 22, 1890. A few years later, the name was changed to Zion Lutheran Church when this photo was taken. During the 1930s, the church was idle until a January 12, 1939, meeting when it was decided to reopen the church. In 1993, it was purchased by Tannenbaum Holiday shops and used for commercial purposes. (Courtesy of the John Blossom Family.)

Future parishioners of the Christ Evangelical Lutheran Church built the church in 1876 before it had a pastor. There was a shortage of pastors, and they had to wait until a graduate from the St. Louis Seminary was available. When Pastor L.F. Huber arrived August 31, he discovered there were no provisions for his stay. A small log house became his temporary quarters, until a parsonage was built in 1877. Services and records were kept in the German language until the 1940s, when English began to be used in both the church and bible classes, which met on Saturdays. The above photo was taken in 1965. After the parsonage was razed in the early 1950s, fish boils were regularly conducted to raise money for a parish hall (shown on the left). In its first century, 545 parishioners were baptized at the church, 346 were confirmed, 188 received a Christian burial, and 101 marriages were performed. According to several parishioners, membership has been "declining for the last 20 years." (Courtesy of the Christ Evangelical Lutheran Church.)

St. Rosalia's Catholic Church in Sister Bay was built in the early 1900s by Henry Seiler, a Jacksonport carpenter. He did all the woodwork, plastering, and finishing work for $150. The church could accommodate one hundred worshippers.

The Catholic community of Sister Bay attended services in the Sister Bay home of Pat Dimond from 1874 to 1879. Mass was celebrated once a month when priests from Baileys Harbor, Institute, and Sturgeon Bay traveled north to Sister Bay. As the congregation grew, services were then conducted in a larger room measuring 18 by 30 feet provided by Andre Roeser. Mass was performed every two weeks with hymns sung in German. Roeser was the first altar boy or mass server, succeeded by his sons. In 1909, Andre and Leone Roeser sold two-thirds of an acre at a cost of $100 to the Green Bay Diocese for the first Catholic church. The deed was signed by Father N. Hunold, OMI, for the church, and by Mrs. Elda Roeser for the congregation. (Courtesy of the Guterman Family Archives.)

Martin Jischke and Mary Bunda were the first couple to be married at St. Rosalia's Church in Sister Bay. The wedding took place on September 14, 1910. Jischke was born in Germany and arrived in the United States when he was nine years old. Bunda was born in Kewaunee, Wisconsin, and came to Door County when she was six months old. The couple lived with the wife's mother, with Mary working at the mother's general store called Bunda's, and Martin working in his dad's meat market in Sister Bay for an annual wage of $25. (Courtesy of George Jischke.)

One of the largest wedding parties in Sister Bay followed the wedding of Sharon Willems to Dick Daubner on October 23, 1971, at St. Rosalia's Church. A new front entrance had been added to the church by this date. More than four hundred people attended the wedding ceremonies at the church and the reception at Hotel duNord. (Courtesy of Sharon Daubner.)

Construction of the new 11,000-square-foot St. Rosalia's Church in Sister Bay began August 1, 1983. The church was built to accommodate the growing population of the immediate church community, as well as the large numbers of vacationers who regularly attend services between May and October of each year. The last expansion of the church occurred in 1956, when seating capacity was increased to three hundred. The new church is designed to seat five hundred during the summer months in sections that can be closed off for the winter. The ceiling has an R-76 rating, and the walls have an R-25 rating to efficiently stave off Door County winters. Jerome J. Koskowski and Associates was the architectural firm, with J.E. Gilson and Company as the general contractor. The total cost for the building project, which includes six classrooms, a meeting room, kitchen, social hall, and the church itself was around $600,000.

There was a pilgrimage of sorts when parishioners of St. Rosalia's Church moved sacred objects and precious mementos from the old church to the new on Sunday, June 24, 1984. Pictured above are the Reverend Paul Stoeckel, Pastor Pat Conlon, and visitors carrying the tabernacle—Jon Conlon and Ed Garzoni. (Courtesy of the St. Rosalia Church Archives.)

Bishop Adam Maida (center) of the Diocese of Green Bay consecrated the new St. Rosalia Church on September 9, 1984. Also pictured in the above image are Rev. Paul Stoeckel (left), pastor of St. Rosalia at the time, and Monsignor John Schuh, master of ceremonies for the dedication. The honor guard was the Fourth Degree of the Knights of Columbus from Baileys Harbor in Door County. All faiths in Door County were represented at dedication services including Jeanne Chase, organist from St. Paul's Catholic Church in Fish Creek, the Trinity Lutheran Church Children's Choir from Ellison Bay, Rev. Ken Okkerse of Christ the King Episcopal Church in Sturgeon Bay, Rev. Dale Hedstrand of Bethel Baptist Church in Ellison Bay, the Men's Choir of the First Baptist Church of Sister Bay, Rev. Jeff Williams of two Lutheran churches in Door County, Rev. Dorothy Mendonca of the Hope United Church of Christ in Sturgeon Bay, and Bernice Koehler, organist of the Ephraim Moravian Church. At the time of the church's dedication, there were about 150 families in the parish. In 1999, there were about 220 families. (Courtesy of the St. Rosalia Church Archives.)

Students in the second grade at St. Rosalia's Church receive their First Holy Communion on the first Sunday in May. Shown above at the altar with Rev. Chester Cappucci, OMI, pastor of St. Rosalia, are, from left to right: Amanda Bonn, Katie Meyer, Jackie Charney, Katelyn Bryzek, and Deborah Smrz. Preparations to receive First Communion include attendance at CCD (Confraternity of Christian Doctrine) classes every Sunday for three years. (Courtesy of the St. Rosalia Church Archives.)

Rev. Chester Cappucci, OMI, celebrates mass at the new St. Rosalia's Church in Sister Bay. Assisting are James Bunda, left, and Danny Smrz, right. Natural fieldstone was selected for the wall behind the altar. The cross is a hand-carved lindenwood crucifix, which was carved in the area of the Italian Alps. A large stained glass window, opposite the wall shown at right, reflects off the ceiling and the textured walls of the church.

Youngsters are active at St. Rosalia's parish community throughout the year. At the present time, there are about 20 active altar boys and girls who assist at Saturday and Sunday masses every weekend. About one hundred students are in the church's regular school in grades from pre-kindergarten to tenth grade. There is also a summer school program for two weeks. Thirty students from Sister Bay and Baileys Harbor attended the summer sessions in 1999. (Courtesy of the St. Rosalia Church Archives.)

Mary Jischke's 100th birthday was celebrated in 1988. Although Mary was born on the 16th of May, she always celebrated her birthday on the 11th. In the above photo, Mary is shown planting a flowering tree on St. Rosalia's Church grounds as she celebrated her birthday. She was expected to throw a shovel of dirt on the tree while it was being held, but she promptly filled the entire hole to the surprise of the onlookers. At the right is Laurence Daubner, Mary's longtime friend, and chairman of building and grounds at St. Rosalia's, who arranged the tree planting. (Courtesy of Emilie Daubner.)

Tonda Gagliardo and Karl Bradley were married May 9, 1998, at the Mission Grille, the former St. Rosalia Church, by Judge Peter Diltz. Tony Gagliardo, father of the bride, is shown congratulating the young couple immediately after the ceremony, which was performed in the restaurant. Notice the large photo reproduction of the first St. Rosalia's Church, which is on permanent display in the restaurant. (Courtesy of Tonda Gagliardo.)

The Transfiguration of Our Lord Chapel incorporated in the Diocese of the Midwest Orthodox Church in America, shown above, was built in Sister Bay under the direction of George (Pat) Mangan, a professional architect. Mangan originated the idea of the chapel as he developed a keen interest in early Christian architecture. He discovered that such small chapels were being built throughout the Middle East under the direction of a church. A unique architectural discovery—the pendentive—made the construction of a dome on a square possible. Mangan secured the blessing for the chapel project from John, Archbishop of Chicago, Diocese of the Midwest of the Orthodox Church in America on October 2, 1975, and secured the approval of the State of Wisconsin as well.

Construction immediately began on the project. Mangan, his family, and his friends worked on the project. The first service, a Divine Liturgy, took place in the chapel in 1980 when Rev. Cyril Lukashanik from the Orthodox Church in Chicago celebrated with other priests. At this time, a wooden floor and a timber frame were in place. The dome was set atop the chapel between 1983 and 1987.

The chapel has been open to the public since the first services in 1980. During Fall Festival, vespers and the Divine Liturgy are served. Many regular visitors from St. Matthew's parish in Green Bay have regularly attended services here since 1983.

Mangan is building a path to the chapel from the main highway in Sister Bay, Route 42, to make it more accessible to visitors. (Courtesy of the Transfiguration of Our Lord Archives.)

Sean Mangan and Sue Chrismer were the first couple to be married in the Transfiguration of Our Lord Chapel in Sister Bay in August 1988. Performing the ceremony was Father Hilary, aide to the Orthodox Bishop in Chicago. (Courtesy of the Transfiguration of Our Lord Archives.)

Father Hilary, aide to the Orthodox Bishop of Chicago, is a frequent guest at the Transfiguration of our Lord Chapel in Sister Bay, which was built and remains in a heavily wooded area. For 14 years, Father Hilary took a bus every weekend for services at St. Matthew's Church in Green Bay. The photo at left shows Father Hilary in the doorway to the chapel before permanent doors were attached. (Courtesy of the Transfiguration of Our Lord Archives.)

Religious icons have been placed and removed in the Transfiguration of Our Lord Chapel, depending on the weather. When the walls were permanently placed in 1989, icons and religious items have remained in the chapel. The Mother of God icon (Alpha) is always on the left in an Orthodox Church, and Christ at the Last Judgment icon (Omega) is always on the right. (Courtesy of the Transfiguration of Our Lord Archives.)

Five

Education

The oldest schoolhouse in Door county was built as a result of a meeting on December 7, 1865. The school district, which included Sister Bay, Appleport, Rowleys Bay, and Wildwood, was organized on that date. The first year's budget was $200. A log cabin schoolhouse was built just north of today's Sister Bay, and classes were conducted until 1881. The above photo shows the schoolhouse building in its new location in Gateway Park at the intersection of Highways 42 and 57, where it serves as an information center for Sister Bay during the summertime.

The original Sister Bay schoolhouse was used for private purposes after 1881, when classes were no longer taught in the building. It was deteriorating during the 1960s when it was deeded to the Door County Historical Society. The schoolhouse was restored as a Bicentennial project and dedicated October 17, 1976, in Sister Bay's Gateway Park at the intersection of Highways 42 and 57. (Courtesy of the Village of Sister Bay.)

The above photo depicts the first Wildwood school, which was launched in the early 20th century on land donated from the Beyers estate. The school was "quite established by 1914," according to a local observer on the date the above photo may have been taken, when all eight grades were in attendance at the school. Students from Sister Bay and Rowleys Bay attended. (Courtesy of Helen Carlson.)

Two teachers of Sister Bay around 1915 are pictured at right—Mayme Witalison Erickson, left, and Alma Witalison Bunda, right. Mayme attended Teacher's Training School in Marinette. (Courtesy of Helen Carlson.)

The Sister Bay School was built in 1909 on top of a hill at the southern end of the village. It served the needs of the village until 1958, when an addition for two rooms was started and then opened for classroom use in 1960. Today, the former school is a daycare center. (Courtesy of the Sister Bay Historical Society.)

The new Wildwood School was opened in 1922 as an elementary school with two sections—one for grades 1–4, the other for grades 5–8. It opened as a high school in 1924, with classes in English, history, science, and algebra in its two-year curriculum. A graduate of the first high school graduating class recalls that there were four students in the freshmen class and four in the sophomore class when she started high school at Wildwood. Many elementary school graduates did not continue with high school at that time. Often the school would close in winter since snowdrifts created high ridges, and students had to walk the 3 miles from areas of Sister Bay. School started at 9:00 a.m. and finished at 4:00 p.m. (Courtesy of Phyllis Larson.)

The Appleport School built at the intersection of Old Stage Road and Highway ZZ, about midway between Sister Bay and Rowleys Bay, accepted its first kindergarten students in 1963. It also held classes for all eight grades and accepted students that previously would have been scheduled to attend Wildwood or the Sister Bay public school.

Six

Social Life and Culture

All types of postal cards, including humorous ones, were mailed in the early decades of the 20th century inviting guests to come to Sister Bay. Even though many, if not most, guests arrived by boat, there must have been many autos of guests in the Sister Bay area considering the amount of service stations. As for those who did not have their own auto, Sister Bay was perhaps the only community in Door County that had its own taxi service. (Courtesy of Allen Erickson.)

This postal card does not state, but implies, "falling in love." Many first-time visitors, going back more than a century, purchased property, and their children and grandchildren have remained frequent visitors to Sister Bay. Much of the literature written by those who chose to come and remain in Sister Bay reflects a "love affair" with the area still in full bloom. (Courtesy of Allen Erickson.)

Dorothy Holmes, pictured above, is shown the first time she visited Sister Bay and the Liberty Park Lodge and Shore Cottages during the 1930s. A view of one of the Sister Bay Islands is visible on the right. Since that time, Holmes has returned almost every year to Sister Bay as have her daughters and her grandchildren. She considers Sister Bay "a great family place" and enjoys the atmosphere and the peacefulness. Over the years, Holmes has said the entire area "has pretty much stayed the same." (Courtesy of the Liberty Park Lodge.)

During the first two decades of the 20th century, the Growerlery was a picnic area located in the area of today's Sister Bay Resort and Marina. Families gathered after church services on Sunday. There was a common tent used for changing clothes for those going swimming. Pitching horseshoes was a favorite, as well as playing baseball in a game pitting the youngsters against the seniors. It is reported that on a special occasion, "mom and dad would even split a beer." (Courtesy of George Jischke.)

The above photo is believed to have been taken around 1890 at the Growerlery public gathering or picnic area in Sister Bay. The photographer who took such photos would send word a few weeks in advance that he was coming. The ladies of the village were excellent seamstresses and would get their "finest" prepared for the formal photo sessions. In the above photo are, from left to right (top): Mrs. Gust Wills, Mrs. Mary Bunda, Mrs. Ole Erickson, Mrs. William Knutson, Mrs. Joe Arle, Mrs. Andrew Johnson, Mrs. Casper Nye, and Mrs. Frank Bunda; (bottom) Mrs. Andre Roeser, Mrs. Frank Jischke, Mrs. Henry Pleck, Mrs. Matt Roeser, Mrs. Pete Lhote(?), Mrs. Charles Magnette, and Mrs. Roode (?). (Courtesy of George Jischke.)

Liberty Park Summer Resort, which opened in 1898 in Sister Bay, Wisconsin, was a favorite stop for passengers who traveled on the Goodrich boats that toured throughout the area for several decades. After guests arrived at Abraham A. Carlson's resort, there was croquet, badminton, Ping-Pong, horseshoes, and tennis. Guests could also fish or play cards. In the early 1900s, Liberty Park guests were on the American Plan—three full-course meals were provided with plenty of snacks. The ice in the tea came from the ice stored in the icehouse in back of the resort from the previous winter. (Courtesy of Allen Erickson.)

The Liberty Park Hotel was opened at the northern edge of Sister Bay around the turn of the century. The section of the building on the left was separated from the entire structure and moved by logs and horses to another location about 200 feet away. From the time it opened until the 1940s, the Liberty Park Hotel provided three meals a day for all guests. (Courtesy of Allen Erickson.)

John and Mary Worachek opened the Liberty Grove Hotel in Sister Bay in 1894. The first floor had a large room for dancing and card playing, a lounge, dining room, and kitchen. There were 13 rooms on the second floor that remained open throughout the year. Also, there were outhouses, a changing cabana for bathers, a wash house, an ice shed, and a small pier. The daughters of the owners and several other girls reportedly formed Sister Bay's first basketball team, playing their games in the hotel's dance hall. (Courtesy of Allen Erickson.)

Gunder Anderson, one of the original settlers in the Sister Bay area around 1870, purchased 108 acres of wild timber along the shores of Little Sister Bay. The price was $412.50, calculated at a rate of 550 bushels of potatoes to be delivered over a three-year period, with small and rotten potatoes to be picked out and the remainder valued at 75¢ per bushel. Gunder signed his signature, and the property became his in 1884. His son, Grant, who was involved in commercial fishing, purchased the property in 1900. In 1911, he sold his fishing business and went into dairy farming. The lodging "business" started in 1918 when the first guests stayed overnight at the farmhouse. Little Sister Resort was built in 1920 as a 17-room lodge constructed to accommodate 45. It was torn down in 1974, and facilities were built to house 65–80 guests. (Courtesy of Helen Carlson.)

Two guests are pictured at the Hotel DuNord in 1925. Guests, who usually stayed for two-week periods, were "usually dressed up," as an author of several articles on the early history of the hotel observed, when they went picnicking, boating, or hiking—the usual activities of guests while at the hotel. The hotel opened in 1916. It was a dream fulfilled for Josephine Anderson, who saw a chalet in France, had plans drawn up for a similar building, and the result became the Hotel DuNord (hotel of the North) in Sister Bay. (Courtesy of Mary Alice Gustafson.)

Guests are pictured at the Hotel DuNord at the north end of Sister Bay around 1923–24, when Alice Carlson (on steps) was a guest. It appears that the photo may have been taken in midday after a luncheon prepared by Chef Gurlie Seaquist, whose culinary preparations were consistently praised as "absolutely outstanding." The menu did not vary greatly—fish on Friday, steak on Saturday, and chicken on Sunday. (Courtesy of Mary Alice Gustafson.)

When the Hotel DuNord was opened in 1916, it had a 15-foot fireplace that was built from stones in the area. While the hotel was open, it was lit at all times. It was a favorite gathering spot for Sunday evening's sing-along, or patriotic programs presented the evening of July Fourth. Many guests who stayed at the hotel would return annually for years to come. In 1978, a newspaper article relates the story of a Mrs. Ben Miles who vacationed in Sister Bay every year since 1913, and for 60 years at Hotel DuNord. The article concluded by stating that Mrs. Miles was looking forward to many future vacations at the hotel. (Courtesy of Mary Alice Gustafson.)

The Hotel DuNord did not survive a late November 1982 fire. The cause of the fire was a faulty electrical switch box that erupted into flames. David Wilke, one of the owners of the hotel, was asleep in a room above the switch box when he was awakened by loud, popping sounds—probably from the aerosol cans that were in the area. He smelled smoke and was greeted with thick spirals of dense smoke when he left his room. By 4:30 a.m., some 65 volunteer firemen from Sister Bay, Liberty Grove, and other communities were battling the blaze, which they got under control by 8:30 a.m. The loss was complete with a value of $1 million. "She died a slow death," said the fire captain, David Jungwirth, since the stout wooden beams refused to collapse as the interior was turned to rubble. One board escaped destruction. Removed when the hotel closed for the season, October 31, it had the following inscription: "This hotel was built in 1915 by Carl Carlson, Elmer Anderson, Bob Carlson, Paul Borg, Chester Hedeen, Ralph Seaquist, and Frank Highlander". The hotel was reopened in 1983. (Courtesy of the Hotel DuNord.)

By the 1950s, the Kellstroms finished the road leading from Highway 42 to their homestead. They began to rent in the main building. Eventually, separate cottages were built and rented. The road in the photo above is currently Sunset Drive. (Courtesy of the Kathy Ray Collection.)

Birchwood Hall was described in a newspaper account as "one of the prettiest summer resort hotels in the entire county—on 400 feet of choice shore property on Beach Road north of Sister Bay." Birchwood Hall was built as a hotel in 1909. It was located in a meadow surrounded by cedars and balsams. The resort became a popular place, as stated in the same newspaper article, "with its long, open front porch, privacy,…fireplace,…simple rooms with iron beds, and three excellent home-cooked meals a day." The hotel, particularly at meal times, became the social center of the area, as many families who lived in the area or were visiting private residences for the summer, would gather at the hotel for the meals provided for $3.50 per person per week. (Courtesy of Mary Alice Gustafson.)

Before the Laura Maxwell Inn was bought out by the Hotel DuNord, it provided 16-20 units to accommodate guests. In 1964, rates were $12 per single person, $8 per double occupancy, and $7 per triple occupancy. A "full regatta" breakfast and dinner added $4.50 daily to a guest's bill. (Courtesy of the Zielke Family Archives.)

Helm's Four Season's Resort started as a business in 1959, when 18 cottages were purchased from Lamb's Resort. These were available between Memorial Day and Labor Day. In 1964, year-round motel units replaced some of the seasonal cottages. Chalet architecture was incorporated in 1970. Later additions in 1991 included conference rooms and a 45-foot indoor pool. (Courtesy of the Zielke Family Archives.)

The Sister Bay Hotel was used for a variety of affairs in early 20th century Sister Bay. The large gathering pictured above at the hotel suggests it was a formal affair with all gentlemen wearing hats and congregating in one area with the women elsewhere. Perhaps the carriage on the right was a bridal carriage that had just dropped off the bride. (Courtesy of Against the Grain Wood Products and Furniture Repair.)

Henry Koepsel purchased the Sister Bay Hotel in 1917–18 and owned it until he passed away in 1938. The above scene depicts the hotel's bar room in the early 1930s. According to a person familiar with Koepsel's ownership of the property, "there was plenty of moonshine sold there." The sheriff "always got a cut" and would "wise them [the owners] up" when the feds were coming around. The feds were there not only to check on the liquor but also on the slot machines that weren't too well-hidden. However, the slots didn't quite bring the bonanza the owners envisioned. One night the cook left the windows open, and all the slot machines were stolen. The bar at the Sister Bay Hotel was well stocked and prepared to serve not only the patrons, but also the workers from the public service company who spent quite a few days at the site when the electrical lines were installed during the 1920s. The bar also provided refreshments for the hundreds of dancers in the hall who came regularly to the hotel for Saturday night dances. (Courtesy of Eldred Koepsel.)

Long dresses and bow ties were apparently the style when this photo was taken at Sister Bay's Liberty Park Lodge in the early 1900s. On the porch are Gustaf Malgren, Helma Carlson Johnson, Myrtle Johnson, Anna Carlson, and Julia Carlson; left of the steps are Abraham Carlson, George Carlson, his son, and Christine Carlson. On the right is Arthur Carlson (son of Abraham). The identity of those on the steps is unknown. Liberty Park Lodge was built in 1898 by Abraham Carlson, who managed the 14-room tourist property with his wife, Christine. (Courtesy of the Liberty Park Lodge.)

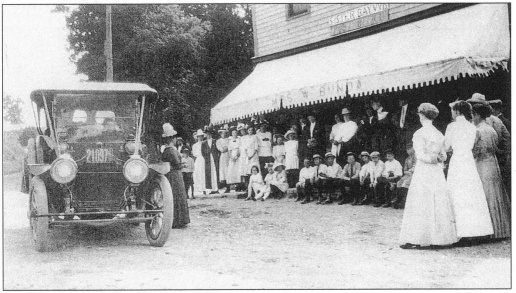

The national movement to gain the right to vote for women came to Sister Bay in 1912. Mrs. Katherine McCullough, a suffrage campaign speaker, urged that women obtain the right to vote in a speech in front of the store of Mrs. W. Bunda. Leona Bunda, who was married to William Berns—mother of Robert Berns, who became very active in the lumber business of Sister Bay—was one of the ladies present in the above photo. (Courtesy of the Robert Berns Collections.)

A Sunday afternoon cruise on Little Sister Bay with all gentlemen wearing their best Sunday hat is pictured above. The cruise usually lasted the entire afternoon with all the islands near Sister Bay visited. The old fish house is in the background, which employed as many as a dozen people at one time, dressing several tons of fish daily. As many as 2 tons were brought in on one lift. Fish were both salted and preserved on ice. When fish were especially plentiful, the iced fish would be stored on trays and taken daily to Chicago. (Courtesy of Helen Carlson.)

An arrival of a Goodrich boat was always a social "highlight" for the entire village, where many people would gather in the dock area and await its arrival. Helen Mills Clark, in an affectionate memoir of her experiences in Door County titled "Where Rings the Dinner Bell," writes: "Thirty years ago the roads were narrow, dusty, unimproved. People arrived at our docks in boats, the old *Carolina* and *Arizona*, landing cargo and passengers alike. It was a leisurely day and a half-trip from Chicago, and the arrival brought everyone to the docks. What fun it was to sit on the dock piles or to dangle one's legs over the water. Excitement was rampant as the hour for the arrival neared. And what a pleasant sight when the vessel turned the bluffs, stately and large as it hove in sight. And what excitement it was to be where friends were hilariously greeted, and trunks were carried on the backs of men to the inns." (Courtesy of Mary Alice Gustafson.)

After the *Carolina* of the Goodrich lines arrived at the Roeser Dock in Sister Bay, most, if not all, the villagers would be there to greet it. The *Carolina* was launched in South Philadelphia in 1892, and the Goodrich Lines purchased it in 1906 for $80,000. The 220-foot vessel was sent to Manitowoc, where it was completely rebuilt. It was then put into service with a regular Chicago to Mackinaw Island summer run with stops in Sturgeon Bay, Fish Creek, Ephraim, Sister Bay, and Washington Island. Shown above are Sister Bay residents Edith Becker, John Pahl, and Mary Starr. (Courtesy of the Robert Berns Collections.)

The above photo is believed to have been taken of a wealthy family vacationing in the Sister Bay area for the summer in the early part of the 20th century. Sister Bay and other locations in Door county were being sought out, since the air was said to be cleaner and healthier. When wealthy families selected a designated vacation area in Door County such as Sister Bay, several large trunks would arrive a week or so earlier than the family. These trunks, and many others that would follow, would have to be transported to the vacation site. The contents would have to be unpacked and made ready for use by the family. Such families often brought their own maids and handymen, as can be seen in the above photo. (Courtesy of the Kathy Ray Collection.)

Although it is unlikely that this group actually did the fishing while they were guests at Liberty Park Lodge during the 1920s, it did not stop them from posing for this photo, as did groups earlier and probably later in the day. Note the uniform of the second gentleman from the left. It appears to be much closer to the dress of a chauffeur than a captain of a fishing boat. (Courtesy of the Liberty Park Lodge.)

After farmers began moving away from property along Green Bay—since it was difficult to farm—members of the North Side Swedish Club of Chicago began purchasing the properties in the 1920s. The charter members of this group established Beach Road, where many of the properties are located even still today. Pictured above, in the summer of 1920, are members of the Ladies Auxiliary of the club: Alice Carlson, Anna Linn and her dog Buster, Jeanette Carlson, Hanna Friedlund, Mrs. Nils Tuveson, and Mrs. Charles Bostrom. The group was staying at the Liberty Park Hotel; however, this meeting occurred in front of today's Door County Ice Cream Factory just north of the hotel. Although the scene suggests the occasion was festive, the reason for all the flowers is unknown. (Courtesy of Mary Alice Gustafson.)

Wenzel Bunda's original residence, built almost a century ago, is shown as the left section of the building above. After Bunda passed away, his wife built the addition on the right (double windows on the first floor, two separate windows on the second) to lodge the frequent visitors who arrived on the Goodrich lines and the workers in the factories along the Green Bay shoreline. The current owner purchased the property in 1944, for $1,500 with 36 payments scheduled at $25 per month. The building was paid off in 22 months since the cherry seasons were bountiful, and the children of the owners were able to pick several hundred buckets at 25¢ a bucket. (Courtesy of Phyllis Larson.)

Three families—the Blossoms, the Greenes, and the Woodwards—each purchased land in Sister Bay from Abraham Carlson in 1909. Each built a sleeping cottage on the 2-acre plot, and have lived in and maintained those properties since that time. Shown above is the "La Maisonnette Fleurie," (The House of Flowers), the Blossom family cottage, which was the first to be built. A kitchen was added in the 1940s. Water pumped from the bay was used for cooking but not for drinking. (Courtesy of the John Blossom Family.)

Claus Haven, one of the properties on Beach Road, in Sister Bay is pictured above. Claus Carlson built the homesite in 1924, and the water tower on the right was installed the same year. Water that was used daily for washing, toilets, and watering the grass had to be pumped daily from Green Bay. Water for drinking and cooking was provided by a well. Claus Haven would be completely closed in September or October and reopened in May, as were most of the homes along Beach Road. The Village of Sister Bay voted to have a sewage system built in the early 1970s. (Courtesy of Mary Alice Gustafson.)

A popular picnic area of Sister Bay residents and guests at the resort hotels in the area was Europe Lake, a few miles north and east of the village. The photo above was taken in 1912 when John R. Greene, seated at left, and Frederick and John D. Blossom, standing on left, arrived there ready for a swim. (Courtesy of the John Blossom Family.)

Sister Bay had its own "Field of Dreams" well before the book and movie became popular years later. Shown here are the "Sister Bays" baseball team against a background of a cornfield. Baseball was very popular in all villages in Door County, with the "big" games usually played on Sunday or on the Fourth of July. The Sister Bays' ballfield was located on the site that later became the Masterfreeze Corporation—today's Walkway shops in the center of the business district. (Courtesy of the Sister Bay Historical Society.)

Two young ladies, Virginia and Caroline Woodward, wait at Pebble Beach on Woodward's dock in the harbor of Little Sister Bay, while Ed King and his friend prepare the rowboat for an afternoon ride on the bay. The vegetation in the background, the wide-brimmed hats the ladies are wearing, and the shadows being cast suggest a bright sunny summer day in 1920 when the photo was taken. What could have been the purpose of the jacket one of the ladies is holding? (Courtesy of Alice Gustafson.)

Members of the Blossom family and friends are pictured on their way to Ellison Bay, about 4 miles north of Sister Bay, for a picnic. The time is around 1915–20. In the background is the Zion Lutheran Church at the northern edge of the Village of Sister Bay. (Courtesy of the John Blossom Family.)

A picnic at Europe Lake, just north and east of Sister Bay, is pictured above. The photo was taken around 1918 and perhaps on the Fourth of July, which, in the words of a person familiar with that time period in Sister Bay history, said "was a really big deal." Notice the informality of those attending the picnic. Neither the gentlemen nor the ladies had their hats on, and almost everyone is wearing short sleeves or has their sleeves rolled up. The menu included the standard baked beans, hamburgers, and potato salad. In the evening, especially on the Fourth of July, there were plenty of sparklers. Camping gear would frequently be taken along, and the picnickers would sleep overnight. (Courtesy of the John Blossom Family.)

Young ladies are preparing for the Sister Bay Regatta by doing their laundry at the end of the Blossom Dock in Sister Bay. The dock was temporary, having to be rebuilt each year since most docks did not survive the long winters when Green Bay froze over. The lady leaning over the dock is Jane Wheeler Schimph. Note the nautical theme in each of the outfits the ladies was wearing. (Courtesy of the John Blossom Family.)

The photo at right is of Regatta Day in Sister Bay in 1915. Men wore their hats, young boys wore knickers, and young ladies wore bonnets and their Sunday best. Nautical events included sailing, rowing, canoeing, and log rolling. (Courtesy of the John Blossom Family.)

The young girls above were dressed for a birthday party at the cottage of the Woodwards, who owned some bay-front property at the north end of Sister Bay. The girls have their dolls, which they proudly show off. The style of clothing, particularly the big bows, was also frequently seen in photos of this same time period—1915–1920—taken at the Swedish Baptist Church of Sister Bay located on the southern end of the village. (Courtesy of the John Blossom Family.)

A typical Sunday afternoon tea party at a private Beach Road residence on a veranda or porch that faced Green Bay is pictured above. During the mid-1920s, when the above photo was taken, in the words of one who has written extensively about the period, "everyone was always giving parties...[the people] were always very social. Everybody was all dressed up (notice the gentlemen in ties, ladies in high heels, young girl with high white socks), and they usually went over to the Hotel DuNord for dinner." (Courtesy of Mary Alice Gustafson.)

An iceboat, probably homemade around the turn of the century, that was used for recreational purposes on Sister Bay is pictured above. The driver, in the words of one who heard about how these boats were used in earlier days, "had to know where he was going" on these boats which achieved speeds of 65 to 70 mph on the ice. The driver, who was in control of the boat, would lie flat in the area where the dog is in the above photo. There were three runners—two rear runners and the steering runner in the front. Standing on the rear runner during a run would depend on how strong the wind was blowing. There probably was considerable traffic on the ice, since some of the more dangerous areas were marked to warn boaters. (Courtesy of the Kathy Ray Collection.)

One of Sweden's major holidays, Midsummer Fest, is regularly celebrated in Sister Bay at Al Johnson's Restaurant on Saturday, June 21, or the closest Saturday to that date. Uniforms are specially made in Sweden for all employees. Performances, dances, and other traditional observances of the day are performed in the restaurant and on the restaurant grounds. (Courtesy of the Zielke Family Archives.)

The above photo was taken during Fall Festival, probably in the late 1950s or early 1960s. The large building on the right is the Masterfreeze Corporation, which was Sister Bay's largest corporation. It was purchased in 1945, and an addition was built in 1946. Masterfreeze manufactured home freezers, walk-in coolers, and milk coolers at the site. By 1961, more additions were built, and the plant occupied 27,000 square feet. (Courtesy of Betty L. Wiltse.)

One of the highlights of the Sister Bay Fall Festival is the traditional Door County fish boil. Believed to have its origins with early Scandinavian settlers in Door County, fresh whitefish were combined with potatoes and onions in a large pot and boiled over an open fire. When the fish are ready, the dramatic "boil over" occurs when kerosene is dumped on the fire. A roaring fire causes the water to "boil over," which carries away most of the fish oils and fat.

The library in the background was built along the beach to accommodate visitors. (Courtesy of the Zielke Family Archives.)

122

This is a typical crowd in Sister Bay during Fall Festival in mid-October. Originally the event was a final meeting of the local townsfolk at the end of summer and harvest season before the long winter would set in. However, over the years, visitors were attracted from many areas swelling the weekend population to perhaps 25,000 for a village of 700 residents. Since many drive in for one day of the festival and must leave the same day because sleeping accommodations are not available anywhere in or near Sister Bay, attendance figures are difficult to estimate. The scene at right is Highway 42 in the central business district of Sister Bay. The one building in view, top left, is the Sister Bay cafe. (Courtesy of the *Door Reminder*.)

The Sister Bay Fall Festival was a gathering of local townspeople at the end of the resort season and after the harvest. Over the years, numerous activities have been added, and thousands of visitors are attracted to Sister Bay. The schedule of events for the 54th festival in 1999 included these attractions: Friday—arts and craft fair, historical tours, fish boils, music by the "Nightlighters," children's cake walk, Irish ghost stores, and fireworks; Saturday—pancake breakfast, parade (shown at left), "Rockin" Jimmy and the Blue Weasels," liars contest, and events repeated from Friday; and Sunday—"Fall Classic Run," soapbox derby, Ping-Pong ball drop, Habitat for Humanity drawing and events repeated from the previous two days. (Courtesy of the *Door Reminder*.)

One of the highlights of the Sister Bay Fall Festival is the Ping-Pong ball drop. A helicopter will fly overhead, usually on the Saturday afternoon of the weekend festival in mid-October. It dumps thousands of Ping-Pong balls on the crowd waiting below on the main business avenue, Highway 42. The balls are valuable, since many contain certificates for merchandise at local merchants or meals at local restaurants. (Courtesy of Lon Kopitzke.)

Henry Beury, a retired lighthouse keeper, was the caretaker of a nature center at Three Springs near Appleport. Started by Harold Wilson in 1949, a concerted effort was made to collect all local animals and have them available for viewing at the nature center. In the photo at left, Beury is displaying fox snakes that are common to the area. (Courtesy of Helen Carlson.)

Edwin H. Casperson of Sister Bay purchased the sleigh funeral coach shown above in 1918, and began using it the same year in the Sister Bay area. It was delivered over the frozen ice of Green Bay from Marinette, Wisconsin. It was used during the winter months, when it was impossible to use motored vehicles for transportation. When in use, the horses pulling the sleigh wore matching harnesses and blankets. Mr. Casperson and the teamster were dressed in black fur coats and caps. The coach was stored in Ellison Bay when not in use. Casperson opened a funeral home in Sister Bay in 1921. (Courtesy of Clyde Casperson.)

A 300-foot-long addition was added to the Sister Bay Marina in 1978, and a slip on the long pier was built a year later. The Sister Bay Marina was completely rebuilt in 1993, with provisions for a minimum of one hundred boats. However, since some of the slips are 60 feet long, as many as 155 boats can be docked. Approximately 35 slips, which include electricity and water, are available for transient boaters. New breakwalls were installed in 1993 along with a new harbormaster building.

One of the highlights of the summer season is the Marina Fest at the Sister Bay Marina, which is usually held on the Labor Day weekend. In 1999, a wooden boat show featured the *Zayra*, a 1972 Trumpy Yacht, one of the last three wooded yachts to be built by Trumpy. *Zayra* weighs 69 gross tons, is 72 feet long, and has a maximum speed of 18 knots. The boat was open for tours to guests attending Marina Fest. "Zayra" is a Russian word that can be translated as "sunrise".

The Anderson House was built in Marinette in the last quarter of the 19th century. It was brought to Sister Bay across the ice of Green Bay in 1895. It was the only house in northern Door County to have a street number and ornate carvings above the windows and other fine architectural touches. Alex and Emma Anderson, with their two children, Ivan and Scione, occupied the house until Alex died in 1915. Emma remarried and left in the 1930s to live in Ohio. The house was occupied for only a few weeks a year after that time, until occupancy ceased in 1952. In 1994, the Sister Bay Village Board bought the property with the intention of tearing it down, and David G. Lee saved it from destruction. He put on a new roof and was able to gather together some volunteers who led to the formation of the Sister Bay Historical Society. The Society restored the building and now manages it as the Old Anderson House Museum. (Courtesy of the Sister Bay Historical Society.)

After the Sister Bay Historical Society gained control of the former Anderson property, it began a restoration process headed by the former president of the Village of Sister Bay, Curt Lindem. Curt, pictured above on the left, is a skilled woodworker and restored the home's ornate window carvings and cornices. Others in the photo are Don Howard, center, and Bill Steger, right. These workers were joined in the restoration effort by Barbara McGivern, Joan Champeau, Eloise Lindem, Dorothea Johnson, and Jim Champeau. John Carlson restored the woodwork to its original condition. Bill Lippert and Tom Sadler have also helped make the Anderson House Museum a reality. (Courtesy of the Sister Bay Historical Society.)

The Anderson House Museum, just south of the Village of Sister Bay on Route 57, was officially opened October 3, 1997. Present for the ribbon-cutting ceremony were: Eloise Lindem, Denise Bhirdo, Village of Sister Bay president, and Marajen Lee. Since 1994, members of the Sister Bay Historical Society attended to its restoration and development as a museum. On display in the museum, which was dedicated August 14, 1996, are 19th century woodworking tools and an oxen yoke owned by Ole Thoreson Lindem, an early settler in the Sister Bay area. There is also a century-old Swedish couch/bed and an antique Monarch cookstove. Some of the personal property of Emma Anderson, who lived in the home more than a century ago, is on display—including a library table, dresser, table, and chairs. (Courtesy of the Sister Bay Historical Society.)

By the fall of 1999, work on the interior of the Anderson House Museum was completed, and a curator, Roberta Kutlik, was appointed. She assembled a staff of volunteers to serve as guides at the museum. Shown above are guides Gloria Berg (left), with Eloise Lindem, and Evelyn Hulbert. After the interior was completed, outdoor artifacts such as the bell from the old Sister Bay schoolhouse and the original Sister Bay mail sleigh have been restored. A project launched in early 2000 involves moving a century old granary and a one-story cottage type building to the property. The two new buildings will be placed on an area of some 6.46 acres adjoining the Anderson House Museum. The Village of Sister Bay purchased this parcel of land for these buildings. Remaining parcels of the newly acquired land will be transformed into a park and picnic area.

9 781531 604554